simply beautiful

rubber stamping

50 QUICK AND EASY PROJECTS

kathie seaverns

NORTH LIGHT BOOKS
CINCINNATI, OHIO
www.artistsnetwork.com

11 10 09 08 07   6 5 4 3 2

Distributed in Canada by Fraser Direct
100 Armstrong Avenue
Georgetown, ON, Canada L7G 5S4
Tel: (905) 877-4411

Distributed in the U.K. and Europe by David & Charles
Brunel House, Newton Abbot, Devon,
TQ12 4PU, England
Tel: (+44) 1626 323200, Fax: (+44) 1626 323319
Email: mail@davidandcharles.co.uk

Distributed in Australia by Capricorn Link
P.O. Box 704, S. Windsor, NSW 2756 Australia
Tel: (02) 4577-3555

Library of Congress Cataloging-in-Publication Data
Seaverns, Kathie.
Simply Beautiful Rubber Stamping: 50 quick and easy projects / Kathie Seaverns.
  p. cm.
Includes index.
ISBN-13: 978-1-58180-792-9 (hardcover: alk. paper)
ISBN-10: 1-58180-792-9 (hardcover: alk. paper)
ISBN-13: 978-1-58180-679-3 (paperback: alk. paper)
ISBN-10: 1-58180-679-5 (paperback: alk. paper)
1. Rubber stamp printing. I. Title

TT867.S43 2005
761--dc22

                    2005000608

Editor: Tonia Davenport
Designers: Leigh Ann Lentz and Kathy Gardner
Layout Artist: Kathy Gardner
Production Coordinator: Robin Richie
Photographers: Al Parrish, Christine Polomsky
Photo Stylists: Janet A. Nickum, Nora Martini

F+W PUBLICATIONS, INC.

metric conversion chart

TO CONVERT	TO	MULTIPLY BY
Inches	Centimeters	2.54
Centimeters	Inches	0.4
Feet	Centimeters	30.5
Centimeters	Feet	0.03
Yards	Meters	0.9
Meters	Yards	1.1
Sq. Inches	Sq. Centimeters	6.45
Sq. Centimeters	Sq. Inches	0.16
Sq. Feet	Sq. Meters	0.09
Sq. Meters	Sq. Feet	10.8
Sq. Yards	Sq. Meters	0.8
Sq. Meters	Sq. Yards	1.2
Pounds	Kilograms	0.45
Kilograms	Pounds	2.2
Ounces	Grams	28.4
Grams	Ounces	0.04

ABOUT THE
author

KATHIE SEAVERNS is an artist, designer and instructor for **JUST FOR FUN RUBBER STAMPS.** She currently presides on the design team of **THE RUBBER STAMPER MAGAZINE** and regularly contributes projects to it as well as other papercraft periodicals. Kathie earned her art degree from James Madison University in Harrisonburg, Virginia. She has experience teaching rubber stampers and stamp store owners in groups as large as one hundred, on topics such as basic rubber stamping, collage, bookmaking, mixed media stamping, artistamps, and novelty cards.

Kathie spent over five years working in a rubber stamp store, learning about the many products and techniques involved in this hobby while assisting customers, teaching classes and attending retail and wholesale conventions. When she's not stamping, she's thinking about stamping!

Kathie lives in Seattle, Washington, with her husband, Dan.

Photo: Dave Mathiesen

DEDICATED TO...

This book is dedicated to my family: my husband, Dan, who patiently listened to me worry about whether or not I could do this project and insisted I could; my son, Dustin, who cheered for me and declared that he wants the first autographed copy; and my daughter, Erin, who stamps with me and tells me how proud she is of my efforts. Thanks to all of you for tolerating the piles of "stuff," the thrown-together dinners and my sometimes scatterbrainedness. I love you all very much.

acknowledgments · My thanks go to Tricia Waddell, who first approached me with the idea of writing a book, and to Christine Doyle, who patiently explained the process. Extra-special thanks go to my wonderful editor, Tonia Davenport (just let me know when you're ready for more of those chocolates!) for encouraging, assuring and helping me along the way as I tackled my first-ever book. Thanks also go to Christine Polomsky, not only for her wonderful photography but for sharing tips with me on digital photography.

I never would have had the opportunity to write this book if it weren't for Debby Drabik and Rick Swoager, owners of Just For Fun Rubber Stamps. Working with them has been wonderful and has created a lasting friendship. Big thanks also go to Sandy Sandrus for her great contributions to this book and her "clever ideas"!

Finally, a group of women who deserve special thanks: the P-nuts, my online e-mail friends who got me to start stamping in the first place. If it weren't for them, I never would have ended up in this wonderful business! Thanks, everybody!

contents

introduction

While working in a rubber stamp store, I became used to hearing customers exclaim "Why, that's simply beautiful!" while looking over the vast array of card samples on display. Those same customers also wished they could find a book of ideas for hand stamped cards and gifts, as ideas were hard to come by. Little did I know then that one day I'd be putting together such a book. As a matter of fact, I never would have dreamed that I would have become involved in this hobby at all!

In 1992, I joined a group of fellow Girl Scout leaders in an online computer group. We bonded and soon discovered that we could share ideas and resources through the magic of the Internet. Gradually, our daughters grew up, but our friendships remained intact. A number of those in our group soon discovered rubber stamping. Before long, nearly the entire group was hooked on rubber stamping, with discussions ranging from techniques to visiting local stamp stores.

Let me tell you, I was a reluctant stamper! With an art degree, I looked at rubber stamps as playthings. What I had observed in large craft stores consisted primarily of cartoon characters that I had no interest in. I'd never been in a specialty stamp store, nor was I motivated to look for one.

Then I started receiving envelopes in the mail that were decorated with colorful inks and lively images. Curiosity got the better of me, and I decided to grab the Yellow Pages and find a rubber stamp store in my neck of the woods.

I discovered that rubber stamps truly are art tools to be used by anyone to create incredible things. With many different companies offering a multitude of images ranging from the very cute to the very sophisticated, there's something to please everyone. And, stamped images are not limited to paper. Thanks to today's variety of inks, rubber stamps can be used on fabric, shrink plastic, glass, ceramic tile, walls and more.

You're about to discover a whole new way to express your creativity. You don't have to be an artist to experience success; rubber stamping is doable by anyone, from the very young to the young at heart!

This book is for those who have never attempted stamping, as well as for those who have plenty of stamping experience. With a variety of projects and ideas, you should find lots of inspiration, whatever your skill level. Enjoy!

materials

I know you're eager to get started in on the projects, but before we do, let's go over some of the basic materials and tools that you will want to have on hand for the ultimate stamping experience.

rubber stamps

Where can you find rubber stamps? Check your phone directory for art and craft retail stores and art rubber stamp stores. The Internet has become a gold mine for stampers! Type "rubber stamping" in any search engine and see what comes up.

Though you may feel overwhelmed the first time you walk into a rubber stamp store, once you understand a bit about the different kinds of stamps, you'll be able to make an informed selection.

Rubber stamps come in all sizes and price ranges. A stamp consists of several layers, beginning with the rubber die, which may be red, brown, gray or any number of colors (and color has nothing to do with quality; rubber is rubber!). You'll want to choose deeply-etched dies that will provide clean, clear images with each stamping. The die sits on a foamy cushion that serves to ensure an even impression. Finally, the die and cushion are mounted on a piece of hard rock maple wood. There is usually a picture of the image on the opposite side of the wood; this is called the *index*. Though usually stamped in black ink, indexes are sometimes color stickers or decals. | **OUTLINED IMAGES** | The images found on rubber stamps can differ in several ways. First are so-called *outline* images, simple, open-designed

images akin to what you would find in a child's coloring book. This type of image lends itself well to embossing and coloring with just about any medium. | **SOLID IMAGES** | Second are bold or solid images. On the stamp's index, these images would appear to be solid black; of course the color of ink you use on this type of stamp will determine its appearance! These stamps are great for applying water-based markers directly to the rubber so that when stamped, the image can be multi-hued. Solid shapes can be used as *shadow* stamps, which have become very popular and can create a multitude of looks with different applications (see the windy leaves card, page 39). | **FINELY-DETAILED IMAGES** | Finally, there are the finely-detailed stamps that may feature elaborate line drawings with lots of cross-hatching and stippling. These images may be embossed with a fine embossing powder referred to as *detail* embossing powder. They also lend themselves well to stamping, colored pencil, watercolor and collage. Usually, the stippling and cross-hatching offer clues to where shading and highlighting should occur when using pencils or paints to color.

ink pads

Ink pads come in a variety of colors, shapes and sizes. Most ink pads have a raised surface, making it easy to ink any size stamp. Re-inkers, for refreshing the ink pads, are available as well. The similarities end there, however, as there are different types of inks for different tasks.

| **EMBOSSING** | Embossing ink pads are spongy pads which may be colorless or slightly tinted a pink or blue (allowing you to see what has just been stamped before embossing). Slow-drying, they are used only for

RUBBER
STAMPS

heat embossing with opaque embossing powders. | **DYE-BASED** | Dye-based ink pads are usually hard felt pads that are saturated with inks made from dyes. They are water-based and come in a wide variety of colors, including a number of *rainbow* pads. Many are acid-free (read the labels). They can be used on glossy or matte papers and will dry very quickly, making them less suitable for embossing. Some dye-based inks are permanent and can be used to stamp images that will be colored in with watercolors or water-based markers, and they can be used for sponging or stippling techniques. | **PIGMENT** | Pigment ink pads are spongy pads that contain the thick, creamy inks created from pure color pigments. They are slow-drying, well suited for heat embossing and blend beautifully when stippled. Pigment inks come in many colors including metallics of gold, copper and silver. The ink washes up easily with water. Included among the pigment inks are the new *chalk* ink pads. They dry to a soft, chalky finish and, unlike other pigment pads, are often quick-drying. It is very important to read the labels. Though many will not dry on glossy or coated cardstocks, there are some that will dry on just about any surface. | **OTHER VARIETIES** | Other inks include those made especially for fabric stamping. Permanent, solvent-based inks and alcohol inks for nonabsorbent surfaces are available as well. Recently, inks that simulate a watermark have been introduced. There are also washable inks, designed for use by children.

embossing powders

These thermographic powders provide, what is to many, the "magic" of rubber stamping! Many colors and textures can be achieved with these powders, including rust, patina and etched metal. | **CLEAR** | Clear embossing powder is a good one to start with. By using a clear powder over colored pigment inks, you can have embossed surfaces in a variety of colors. | **GLITTERED** | These powders add sparkle to your work. There are many such powders to choose from, but you can mix your own by adding equal parts embossing powder to fine glitter. There are also powders that consist of mostly glitter; these are called *tinsels* and are not completely opaque. Be sure to use a colored pigment ink with tinsels in order to have an opaque result. | **METALLIC AND OTHERS** | Also popular are the embossing powders in gold, silver and copper as well as many other different colors and textures. *Detail* embossing powders are extra-fine and are excellent to use with highly detailed images.

adhesives

You will want to have a variety of adhesives on hand when working on your rubber stamp projects. Different types of adhesives perform different tasks, and it's best not to rely on one type of adhesive to serve all of your gluing or attaching needs. | **DOUBLE-STICK TAPE** | Double-stick tape, as the name implies, is sticky on both sides and makes quick work of adhering parts of a card together. I admit to being partial to double-stick tape, because I hate waiting for glue to dry! Foam tape, a dimensional version of double-stick tape, adds interesting depth to your piece. | **GLUE STICK** | Glue sticks are useful for adhering decorative papers to book or journal covers. They go on smoothly and dry quickly. Some glue sticks are colored when wet, but become clear when dry. | **CRAFT GLUE** | A general, all-purpose craft glue can serve most of your embellishment needs, but there are also specialized craft glues available for gluing special items together, such as shrink plastic, metal charms or other surfaces. | **GLUE DOTS** | Glue dots are sticky dots of adhesive, usually on a paper roll, and are easy to use with no wet mess. They work best for small pieces or areas that don't require too much in the way of holding power.

cutting tools

Everyone has their favorite way of cutting paper, and today there are so many tools available to make that task quick and easy. From scissors that give your cuts a fancy pattern to punches that really save time on the cutting of shapes. I rely on all of the following when working on my projects, and if you haven't used some of these tools before, trust me when I say they all have a way of making life easier. | **DECORATIVE-EDGED SCISSORS** | Decorative-edged scissors add interest and class to layers of cardstock. A favorite is the deckle edge, which simulates a torn paper edge. Other popular patterns are scallops and pinking edges, but you'll find dozens of different patterns to choose from. | **DECORATIVE PUNCHES** | Decorative punches come in an unbelievable number of patterns and shapes. Good basics to start with are circle and square punches in a variety of sizes. | **CRAFT KNIFE** | A craft knife and cutting mat will come in handy for detail cutting that scissors just can't reach. Be sure to change the blades of the knife frequently for best results. | **SCISSORS** | Scissors, naturally, are necessary for cutting tasks. For detail cutting, a small pair may be more comfortable to work with; otherwise, choose a good quality pair for regular paper cutting.

HOLE PUNCH

| **STANDARD HOLE PUNCHES** | These punches come either as hand-held versions or they can be found as die punches that you use with a hammer and a protective surface such as a cutting mat. Available in several sizes, the $\frac{1}{16}$", $\frac{1}{8}$" and $\frac{1}{4}$" (2mm, 3mm and 6mm) sizes are the most common.

ways of adding color

There are many choices of coloring media available in local art and craft stores, as well as rubber stamp stores. Listed here are some of the more popular ones and the ones that we'll be using in this book. | **MARKERS** | Many stampers start out with water-based markers as their coloring medium. Dual-tipped markers, featuring two tip sizes, are readily available and come in many colors. Markers may be used not only to color in your work but may also be applied directly to a rubber stamp to provide a multicolored stamped image. They may also be used with colorless blender pens to simulate a watercolor look. | **COLORED PENCILS** | Colored pencils are wonderful to work with and lend themselves to a number of techniques. Choose *artist-quality* pencils, as opposed to the *student* variety and you'll enjoy richer color and easier application. A good, basic set of 12 colors can be your starting point; add more colors from open stock displays as you need them. | **WATERCOLORS** | Watercolor paints lend themselves very well to rubber stamping. Again, choose an artist-quality set as opposed to sets designed for children, which contain many fillers and a smaller amount of pigment. I always recommend that watercolor paints be applied to watercolor paper as opposed to cardstock. Inexpensive pads of lightly-textured cold-pressed watercolor paper readily accept stamp images that do not feature a great deal of detail. | **MICA POWDERS** | These fine powders are available in a wide range of iridescent colors from the very subtle to the very bold. The powders can be applied dry to a prestamped surface or mixed with water to create a watercolor paint. You'll love the shimmer they add to your work! | **CHALKS** | If you wish to have softer, more subtle color, try chalks. You'll find them in sets of solid sticks, as pastel pencils, or pressed into little palettes. They may be applied with cotton swabs, makeup applicators or your finger. After coloring in your artwork with chalks, you may want to spray it with a workable fixative or a clear acrylic spray to keep the color from smearing.

paper

This is where many stampers confess a special weakness. There is such a huge variety of beautiful and unique papers and cardstocks that many of us become paper hoarders, buying them and stashing them away! Papers and cardstocks can be found in art supply stores, rubber stamp stores, scrapbook stores, stationery stores, office supply stores, card shops and stores that specialize in selling nothing but paper products. You will find delicate handmade papers, patterned papers, colorful cardstocks, translucent vellums, wonderful textures, shiny metallics and glossy-surfaced papers. All of these papers come in a variety of sizes and weights, from lightweight text-type paper to heavy cardstock. It is common to find packs of cards precut and prescored for folding, along with envelopes to match. There are even die cut cards featuring windows, pop-ups or other unique shapes for special results. These types of packaged cards can be found in arts and crafts and rubber stamp stores.

other tools

As you become more involved in stamping, you'll discover more tools to make certain tasks easier and more enjoyable. Though not absolutely necessary for success, they're nice to have. | **BONE FOLDER** | A bone folder is an amazingly simple tool that is used for scoring, folding and burnishing papers. Several styles and sizes are available. | **METAL RULER** | A 12" (30cm) metal ruler, with a cork backing to prevent slipping, will not only

HEAT GUN

provide measurements for you, it will be invaluable when using a bone folder to score paper or when using a craft knife to cut straight lines. | **HEAT GUN** | A heat gun (sometimes referred to as an embossing gun) is for use when heat embossing. Caution! This appliance is not akin to your hair dryer! It heats up much hotter, and it will melt embossing powders more quickly (and more safely!) than using stove tops, irons, light bulbs or toasters as a heat source. | **STAMP POSITIONER** | I must admit, a stamp positioner is one of my favorite accessories. This handy tool makes it possible to stamp an image exactly where you want it—no guessing and no eyeballing! | **PAPER TRIMMER** | A guillotine-type paper cutter, a rotary cutter or a personal paper trimmer makes the job of cutting papers and cardstocks much easier. You can find paper cutters in all price ranges.

STAMPS

techniques

Now that you're familiar with the basic materials needed for rubber stamping, there are a few tips and techniques that will be worth a quick mention. After learning the basics, you'll be more than ready to start on the projects that follow. Remember, the goal is to have fun, so don't worry if you don't get everything right on the first try.

inking up a stamp

There are two basic methods of applying the ink to the stamp: tapping the stamp onto the ink pad or tapping the ink pad onto the stamp.

TAPPING THE STAMP ONTO THE INK PAD

one · Tap the stamp lightly against the surface of the ink pad several times. Dye ink pads are firm felt pads while pigment ink pads are spongy, so they will feel different. Don't feel like you have to "squish" the stamp down onto the pad.

two · Press the stamp against your card firmly without rocking it back and forth, to get a clean impression. Then, lift the stamp straight up off of the paper.

TAPPING THE INK PAD ONTO THE STAMP

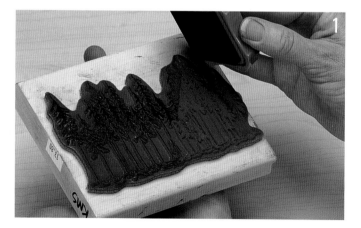

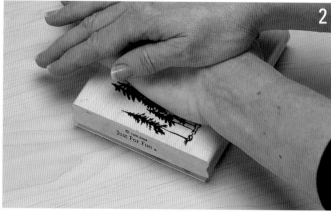

one · For large stamps, such as background stamps, it is easier to leave the stamp on the table or hold it in your hand die side up, and tap the ink pad onto the stamp. You can see how much ink is being applied with this method and where you might need to go back and apply more.

two · With a large stamp such as this one, it is often helpful to stamp while standing and lean your weight into it to exert even pressure.

using a stamp positioner

This handy tool will make it possible for you to place your stamped images exactly where you want them. A stamp positioner will also make it possible to restamp images that did not stamp clearly the first time, allowing you to fix any mistakes. You may feel just a little awkward at first, as you learn the "dance," but before long you'll be an expert with this tool.

one • Line up the imaging plate against the handle, being sure the plate fits exactly in the corner. Align your preinked stamp snugly against the corner of the handle and stamp directly onto the imaging plate.

two • Place the now-stamped imaging plate on top of your card and move it around until it is exactly where you want it. Here, I've already stamped the hand image on my card once; now I want to stamp it a second time so that the fingers are touching each other. Place the positioner's handle back against the plate.

*tip > Baby wipes are a great product to use for cleaning off inked stamps. It's a good idea to clean your stamps as soon as you're done using them. Gently rub the surface of the stamp with the baby wipe to remove the ink. There is no need to rinse the stamp afterwards.

three • Holding the handle securely in place, remove the imaging plate and set it aside. Align the stamp back in the handle's corner and stamp your image directly on your card.

four • Your image should now appear exactly where you want it to be!

adding embossing powder

Get ready; this is where the magic begins! Heat embossing will transform an ordinarily flat stamped picture into a stunning, raised image. Before you begin, make sure your hands are clean and dry and free of any oils or lotions. Damp or oily hands leave fingerprints that attract stray bits of powder.

 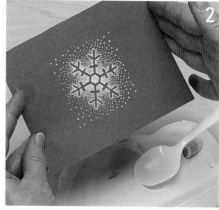 

one · Stamp any image with either embossing ink or a slow-drying pigment ink. Immediately spoon or pour the embossing powder over the wet ink.

two · Tap off the excess powder onto scrap paper or into a plastic container. If you use scrap paper, funnel the excess back into the original container. A tap on the back of the card will remove most stray bits of powder. Any other strays can be brushed away with a fine, dry paintbrush.

three · Turn on your heat tool and direct it to the image. As you see the powder melt, keep the heat tool moving to avoid scorching the paper.

adding color to stamped images

Coloring in your stamped images is fun and may bring to mind those carefree childhood days of coloring in a coloring book! Unlike those days, you have more options when it comes to coloring methods. Here are three quick ways to add color to your work.

STIPPLING, TWO WAYS

one · Stippling will fill in backgrounds with soft color that can resemble air-brushing. One method of stippling is with quick, up-and-down tapping motions with a brush. Tap the brush onto the ink pad, then, in quick strokes, tap the brush onto the paper.

two · To achieve a softer look, apply the color from the brush in a circular motion. Tap the brush onto the ink pad and use smooth, circular motions with the brush to apply color.

WATERCOLOR WITH A WATERBRUSH

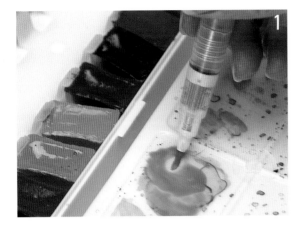

tip > When using any type of moisture (such as water and watercolors) to color in your images, it's important to start with an image that's been stamped in permanent ink to avoid running or bleeding.

one • A waterbrush is special because it contains its own water supply! After filling it with water, squeeze the barrel of the brush to begin the flow of water and pick up a fair amount of paint onto the brush. Make a puddle of paint on your palette. You may mix several colors together during this step, if desired.

two • Blot off any excess paint or water on a paper towel and apply color to the stamped image. Work quickly and avoid "scrubbing" the paint onto the paper. Blend two colors directly on the paper by wiping all paint off the brush and just use clear water to pull the colors together. Wipe the brush off occasionally if there is too much water.

SHADING WITH COLORED PENCILS

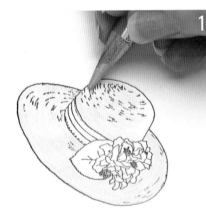

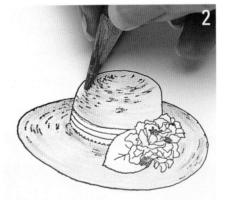

one • To get nice, even tonal areas of color, begin with a dull point on your pencil and keep your strokes light and even, going in either a back-and-forth motion or by using small, light, circular strokes. It's much easier to add more color than it is to take color away. By starting out lightly, you can add additional layers of color, if you would like to.

two • Add a second layer of color on top of the first; this will eventually make all colors intensify.

three • A third layer of color has been added here. Pay attention to areas where shadows occur. This helps to "model" the image and make it more dimensional.

tip > The amount of pressure exerted on a colored pencil will greatly affect the lightness or darkness of the color. A dull tip on the pencil will also result in broader strokes, which can be desirable for filling in larger areas. Use sharpened points for fine detail work.

everyday celebrations

Y ou don't need an excuse to celebrate; everyday occasions are reason enough for handmade cards. Expect to hear exclamations from your friends and relatives as they admire your work and ask you again and again, "Did you really make this?" Just smile and nod. There really is no need to tell them how easy it was! That can be your secret.

Each of the projects in this chapter are easy to make and cover a number of different techniques, such as heat embossing, layering, masking, interesting folds, simple pop-ups and more! Remember to keep in mind that this is not rocket science and you are not a machine—so don't think every single thing you do must be perfect. However, mistakes are often easy to hide by stamping another image here, or gluing down a bow or a charm there. Part of the fun of creating a handstamped card is the fact that there really are no mistakes!

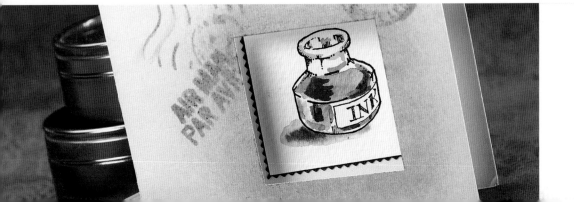

swirl-in-hand card

MATERIALS

RUBBER STAMPS

Torn Paper Design Block,
2-Sided (Just For Fun)

Script Background (Inky Antics)

Swirl-in-Hand (angi-b & co.)

Ivy Border (Alias Smith & Rowe)

INK PADS

Starfish Green, Sea Shells (Ranger)

Deep Lilac, Marvy Matchable
No. 61 (Uchida)

Violet, ColorBox (Clearsnap)

OTHER ITEMS

double-stick tape

6" (15cm) sheer olive ribbon

PAPER
PREPARATION

2" x 2" (5cm x 5cm)
white cardstock

2¹/₂" x 2¹/₂" (6cm x 6cm)
reddish-purple cardstock

2³/₄" x 2³/₄" (7cm x 7cm)
dark green cardstock

5¹/₂" x 8¹/₂" (14cm x 22cm)
pale green cardstock

With a couple of layers and a simple background, this card assembles easily and is great for a first-time effort at stamping. The little touch of ribbon is a simple embellishment and could easily be replaced with a charm or another panel of cardstock with "Happy Birthday" stamped on it!

one · Stamp the smaller square from the 2-sided Torn Paper Design Block on the center of the square white cardstock using Starfish Green ink. Stamp the Script Background on top of this with the Deep Lilac ink.

two · Stamp the Swirl-in-Hand in the center of the square, using the Violet pigment ink. Use double-stick tape to adhere this piece to the reddish-purple cardstock and then adhere that to the dark green cardstock.

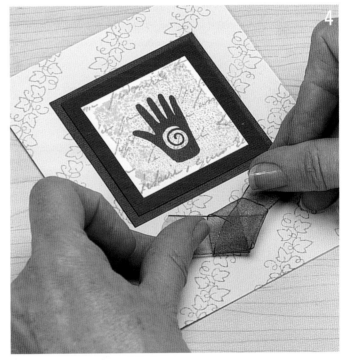

three · Fold the pale green cardstock in half. Ink up the Ivy Border with the Starfish Green ink and, beginning in the center of the front panel, position the image diagonally across the front of the card. Make parallel stampings of the Ivy Border working from the center to the top corner.

four · Repeat with more Ivy Border images, working from the center to the bottom corner. With double-stick tape, layer the hand piece to the top center of the front of the card. Tie the olive ribbon in a loose overhand knot and use a small piece of double-stick tape to adhere it to the lower half of the card.

floral blocks card

MATERIALS

RUBBER STAMPS
Heart Branch Block (Alias Smith & Rowe)
Background 2 Cube (Just For Fun)

INK PADS
Clear Embossing, Top Boss (Clearsnap)
Starfish Green, Sea Shells (Ranger)
Tropical Raspberry, Sea Shells (Ranger)

OTHER ITEMS
white embossing powder
heat gun
deckle-edged scissors
foam tape
double-stick tape

PAPER PREPARATION
$2^7/_{16}$" x $4^7/_8$" (6cm x 12cm)
light green cardstock

2 pieces of $2^1/_2$" x $2^1/_2$" (6cm x 6cm)
light green cardstock

$5^1/_2$" x $8^1/_2$" (14cm x 22cm)
white cardstock

H ere's a chance to try your hand at heat embossing! This card will create a textured background through repeated stampings from a cube stamp. We'll also be using some foam tape to create eye-catching dimension.

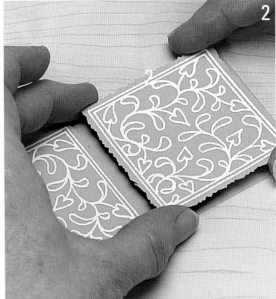

one · Use the clear embossing ink to stamp the Heart Branch Block on each of the light green cardstock squares. Emboss each one with white embossing powder, using the heat gun (see *adding embossing powder*, page 14). Trim the edges of each block with the deckle-edged scissors leaving about 1/8" (3mm) border around each piece.

two · Apply foam tape to the back of each trimmed piece and mount both of the blocks on the larger piece of light green cardstock.

three · Fold the white cardstock in half. Using Starfish Green ink and the "flecks" side of the Background 2 Cube, stamp repeatedly around the edges of the card. It's not necessary to stamp the center because it will be covered with the green piece. Use the Tropical Raspberry ink and the "stipple" side of the cube to repeat the stampings.

four · Apply double-stick tape to the back of the layered green piece and then center and adhere it to the front of the stamped card.

snail card

MATERIALS

STAMPS

Snail Sketch (Just For Fun)

Sketchy Grid (Just For Fun)

INK PADS

Graphite Black, Brilliance (Tsukineko)

Perfect Medium, Perfect Pearls (Ranger)

OTHER ITEMS

clear embossing powder

heat gun

waterbrush or paintbrush

Twinkling H2O's paints (LuminArte, Inc.): Sunflower, Key Lime, Pink Azalea, Bougainvillea, Ocean Wave

double-stick tape

stamp positioner (EK Success)

Perfect Pearls Powders (Ranger): Interference Green, Sunflower Sparkle, Interference Blue

dry paintbrush

soft facial tissue

double-stick tape

PAPER PREPARATION

2⅝" x 3" (7cm x 7cm) watercolor paper

Square Die Cut overlay card (The Paper Cut)

Sparkle and shimmer are bonus features on this window card. By painting with sparkling watercolor paints and brushing on iridescent mica powders, the simple snail takes on some glamour! Using special die-cut window cards with overlays makes it easy to create something very special.

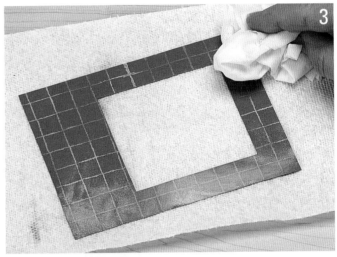

one · Stamp the snail onto the watercolor paper with the Graphite Black ink and emboss with clear embossing powder, using the heat gun. Use the waterbrush and the Twinkling H2O's to color in the snail (see *watercolor with a waterbrush*, page 15). Be brave! Make him colorful!

two · Using double-stick tape, adhere the colored snail piece to the inside of the card, centering it through the window. With the stamp positioner (see *using a stamp positioner*, page 13), stamp the Sketchy Grid onto the overlay cardstock using the Perfect Medium pad. You will need to position the grid stamp twice to completely cover the overlay. With a soft, dry brush, begin brushing on the Perfect Pearl powders, which will adhere to the Perfect Medium. Keep each color distinct and avoid mixing them together.

three · With a soft facial tissue, gently rub off the excess powder. Continue until all the residue is wiped off the overlay. You may fear it will smear, but it won't—honest!

four · Apply double-stick tape to the back of the overlay, including the edges around the window. Center it over the front of the card to finish.

ink bottle card

MATERIALS

STAMPS
Ink Well (Just For Fun)

Antique Pen (Just For Fun)

Air Mail (Just For Fun)

Paris IX (Just For Fun)

INK PADS
Jet Black, Staz-On (Tsukineko)

Stonewashed, Adirondack (Ranger)

OTHER ITEMS
waterbrush or watercolor brush

Twinkling H2O's paints (LuminArte):
Sky Blue, Ocean Wave, Bougainvillea

mini zig-zag decorative-edged scissors

1⅝" (4cm) square punch

stipple brush

double-stick tape

PAPER PREPARATION
2" x 2" (5cm x 5cm) watercolor paper

2½" x 2½" (6cm x 6cm)
pearlescent dark blue cardstock

5½" x 8½" (14cm x 22cm)
pearlescent light blue cardstock

There's no need to struggle with a craft knife—put a punch to work to create your own window card! With all the shapes and sizes of punches available today, it's easy to come up with your own unique window card and you can position a window anywhere you want to.

one · Stamp the Ink Well onto the watercolor paper with the Jet Black ink and color it in using the waterbrush and the Twinkling H2O's. Mount the painted bottle to the small piece of dark blue cardstock and trim closely with the mini zig-zag scissors.

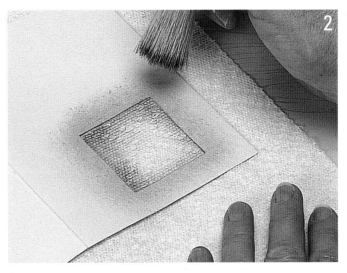

two · Fold the light blue cardstock in half. Punch a square out of the bottom right corner of the card front, inserting the card into the punch as far as it will go. Stipple the Stonewashed ink around the punched opening, keeping the color more intense around the window opening and gradually fading it out toward the edges of the card. (For more on stippling, see page 14.)

three · With the Stonewashed ink, randomly stamp the Antique Pen, Air Mail and Paris IX over the front of the card.

tip > Children's stubby paintbrushes can be used as stipple brushes. Dedicate a stipple brush to each color family so that you don't need to wash the brushes out every time you use them. This will also keep the brushes from contaminating your ink pads with a contrasting color.

four · Apply double-stick tape to the back of the ink bottle piece and adhere it to the inside of the card so that it can be seen through the window.

daisy tri-fold card

MATERIALS

STAMPS
Daisy (Just For Fun)

INK PADS
Graphite Black, Brilliance (Tsukineko)

OTHER ITEMS
clear embossing powder

heat gun

scissors

water-based markers
(American Tombow)

PAPER PREPARATION
Tri-fold card (The Paper Cut)

Take a ready-made tri-fold card and turn it into something unique! This card would make a great get-well or "thinking of you" card for a special person. Subscribing to the "less is more" philosophy of coloring, and using simple water-based markers, you can see how just a touch of color brightens it up!

one · Fold the tri-fold card accordion-style and lay it flat. Using the Graphite Black ink, begin stamping daisies in a row that starts in the bottom left corner and proceeds to the top right corner. Vary the direction of the flower as you stamp. After stamping one or two of the flowers, sprinkle on the clear embossing powder and heat to melt with the heat gun. Fill in the white space on the right side with two or three more daisies.

two · Cut around the top of the daisies, leaving a generous border. Fold the card accordion-style and, in the empty space visible in the center panel, stamp and emboss two more daisies (this will be on the back of the center panel).

three · Begin adding color to the daisies with the markers. Use only quick "flicks" of color, following the contours of the petals. Start with yellow on about half of the flowers, and then add a few lines of peach over the yellow areas.

four · For the other half of the flowers, use pink marker followed by purple. Color all of the flower centers with peach, accented with brown. Finally, color in the stems with green.

joyful leaper card

MATERIALS

STAMPS

Jumpin' (angi-b & co.)

INK PADS

Graphite Black, Brilliance (Tsukineko)

OTHER ITEMS

clear embossing powder

heat gun

waterbrush or watercolor brush

Twinkling H20's paints (LuminArte): Sunflower, Orange Peel, Pink Azalea, Key Lime, Sky Blue, Bougainvilla

scissors

foam tape

PAPER PREPARATION

3" x 7" (8cm x 18cm) watercolor paper

2⁷/₈" x 4⁷/₈" (7cm x 12cm) turquoise cardstock

3¹/₁₆" x 5¹/₁₆" (8cm x 13cm) bright yellow cardstock

5¹/₂" x 8¹/₂" (14cm x 22cm) bright red cardstock

Jump for joy! This colorful card would be especially appropriate for someone who has just landed a new job, gotten a promotion or graduated from school. Bright, shimmering watercolors and colorful cardstocks set the tone for excitement!

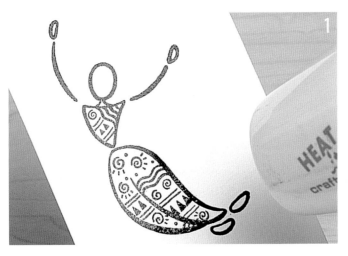

one · Stamp the figure with the Graphite Black ink onto the watercolor paper. Heat emboss with clear embossing powder (see *adding embossing powder,* page 14).

two · Begin adding color with the Twinkling H2O's, using the waterbrush. Start with the lighter colors first and blend in the darker colors as you go. Have fun with the color and don't worry too much about which color goes where.

three · Cut out the painted figure with scissors, leaving a white border around it.

four · Apply pieces of foam tape to the back

five · Layer the figure onto the turquoise cardstock and then onto the yellow cardstock. Fold the red cardstock in half, then finish by layering the yellow piece onto the front of the red card.

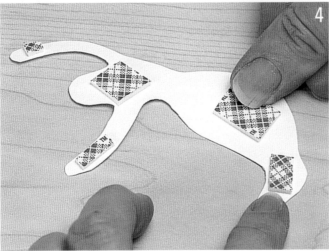

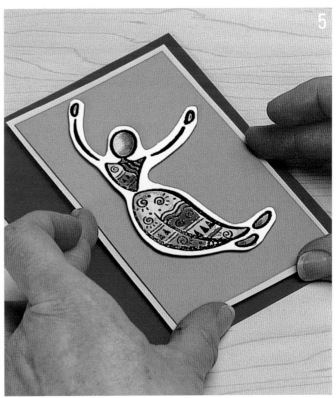

tulip faux-post card

MATERIALS

STAMPS

Large Circle Faux Post (Just For Fun)

Large Circle Faux Post template
(Just For Fun)

Tulip (Just For Fun)

Tulip Silhouette (Just For Fun)

INK PADS

Jet Black, Staz-On (Tsukineko)

Peach Pastel, Fluid Chalk,
ColorBox (Clearsnap)

Rouge, Fluid Chalk,
ColorBox (Clearsnap)

Frost White,
ColorBox (Clearsnap)

OTHER ITEMS

removable tape

sticky notes

scissors

stipple brush

stamp cleaner or baby wipe

colored pencils

stamp decorative-edged scissors

foam tape

double-stick tape

PAPER PREPARATION

3" x 3" (8cm x 8cm)
white cardstock

3" x 3" (8cm x 8cm)
lime green cardstock

5½" x 5½" (14cm x 14cm)
medium blue cardstock

Artists have been creating their own faux postage (also called *artistamps*) for years, making wonderful miniature pieces of art. The rubber stamping world has the tools and the techniques to make this art form easy to do, and the results are simply beautiful!

one · Stamp the faux post circle on the white cardstock with the Jet Black ink. Lay the template over the circle so that the dotted line is covered. Secure with removable tape at the top. Ink up the Tulip stamp with Jet Black and press firmly onto the template and white cardstock.

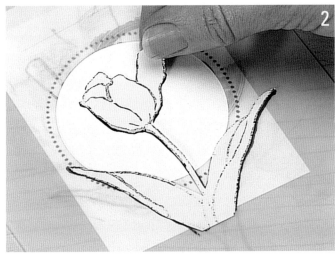

two · Stamp the tulip onto a sticky note and cut it out to make a mask. Place the mask over the stamped tulip.

three · With the mask in place, begin stippling Peach Pastel around the center of the circle opening, using the stipple brush. Next, add Rouge with the stipple brush around the outside area of the circle, blending the two colors together.

four · Remove the sticky note mask and the template. Clean the template with stamp cleaner or a baby wipe. Use colored pencils to add color to the tulip.

five · Cut out the faux postage with the stamp scissors, keeping the blades fairly close to the stamped dotted line.

six · Adhere the cutout postage to the lime green cardstock with foam tape.

seven · Fold the medium blue cardstock in half to make a card. Stamp the Tulip Silhouette with Frost White ink over the front of the card. Keep the stampings random, but be sure to allow some of the tulips to run off the edge of the card. Don't worry about the center of the card; it won't be seen.

eight · Using double-stick tape, adhere the green tulip piece to the upper portion of the card front.

classic daisy card

MATERIALS

STAMPS

Classic Daisy (Just For Fun)

Daisy (Just For Fun)

INK PADS

Yellow, Marvy Matchable No. 5
(Uchida of America)

Orange, Marvy Matchable No. 7
(Uchida of America)

Yellow-Green, Marvy Matchable No. 52
(Uchida of America)

Jet Black, Staz-On (Tsukineko)

OTHER ITEMS

colored pencils: yellow, orange and red

mini zig-zag decorative-edged scissors

double-stick tape

PAPER PREPARATION

$4^3/4$" x $3^1/2$" (12cm x 9cm)
white cardstock

$2^1/2$" x $2^1/2$" (6cm x 6cm)
white cardstock

$2^3/4$" x $2^3/4$" (7cm x 7cm)
lime green cardstock

4" x $5^1/2$" (10cm x 14cm)
dark orange cardstock

$5^1/2$" x $8^1/2$" (14cm x 22cm)
light orange cardstock

one · With the yellow ink, stamp the Classic Daisy in a loose checkerboard pattern on the larger piece of white cardstock. Fill in the alternate spaces with the same stamp using orange ink. Then stamp the Classic Daisy in the remaining spaces with the yellow-green ink.

This simply beautiful little card goes together very quickly. It's perfect for those times when you're planning on meeting a friend for lunch and suddenly remember it's her birthday, or if you just need a quick card.

two · Stamp the larger daisy image onto the $2^1/2$" (6cm) square of white cardstock with the Jet Black ink, then color in the image with colored pencils. Layer the colored image onto the lime green cardstock and trim closely with the mini zig-zag scissors. Layer the trimmed piece onto the center of the stamped background piece.

three · Layer the background piece onto the dark orange cardstock and trim again with the zig-zag scissors. Fold the light orange cardstock in half, then finish by layering the trimmed piece onto the front of the light orange card.

corner leaf card

MATERIALS

STAMPS

Branch Border (Alias Smith & Rowe)

Dandelion, Large (Just For Fun)

Dandelion, Small (Just For Fun)

Maple Leaf, 2-sided (Just For Fun)

INK PADS

embossing ink

Sea Grass, Sea Shell (Ranger)

Bottle, Adirondack (Ranger)

OTHER ITEMS

ruler

bone folder

stamp positioner (EK Success)

gold embossing powder

heat gun

double-stick tape

PAPER PREPARATION

5½" x 8½" (14cm x 22cm)
dark green duplex cardstock

2" x 2" (4cm x 4cm)
light green cardstock

2¼" x 2¼" (6cm x 6cm)
gold metallic cardstock

This particular card uses duplex cardstock—that is, cardstock that has a different color on each side. Choose a duplex cardstock that features a light color on one side and a deeper, contrasting color on the opposite side. A simple corner fold makes it unique!

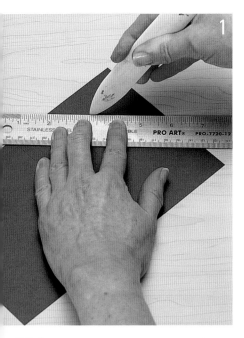  

one · Fold the duplex cardstock in half so that the light side is the inside of the card. Measure 2³/₄" (7cm) from the top right corner toward the fold and again toward the bottom of the card, and mark each spot with an indent, using the bone folder. Use a ruler to connect these two marks, and score a diagonal line from point to point with the bone folder.

two · Use embossing ink and repeatedly stamp the Branch Border in vertical lines across the front of the card. Use a stamp positioner to help with placement, especially when you need to stamp the border twice to fill a vertical line. Keep stampings just under the diagonal fold line, as shown. Add gold embossing powder to the ink and then melt with the heat gun.

three · Open the card up flat and stamp both inside panels with the two dandelion stamps, using the Sea Grass ink. Stamp about five times with the larger dandelion stamp and then fill in with the smaller stamp. Be sure to run some of the images off the edges of the card.

four · Stamp the solid Maple Leaf image on the light green cardstock square, using Bottle ink. Let this ink dry thoroughly (using your heat gun on it will hurry up the drying time), then use the stamp positioner to stamp the vein side of the Maple Leaf stamp using embossing ink. Add gold embossing powder over the veining and melt it with the heat gun. Mount this piece on the square of gold cardstock. Fold the scored corner on the front of the card forward and burnish it with the bone folder.

five · Apply double-stick tape to the back side of the leaf piece and adhere it to the folded section in the top corner of the card. The top left and bottom right corners of the leaf piece should be right on the fold.

leaf twist card

MATERIALS

STAMPS

Maple Leaf, 2-Sided (Just For Fun)

Oak Leaf, 2-Sided (Just For Fun)

Bug Mini-Cube (Just For Fun)

INK PADS

Peach Pastel, Fluid Chalk, ColorBox (Clearsnap)

Key Lime, VersaMagic (Tsukineko)

Ice Jade, Fluid Chalk, ColorBox (Clearsnap)

Stream, Adirondack (Ranger)

Turquoise Gem, VersaMagic (Tsukineko)

OTHER ITEMS

stamp positioner (EK Success)

ruler

bone folder

1/8" (3mm) hole punch

sheer orange ribbon

double-stick tape

PAPER PREPARATION

3$\frac{1}{2}$" x 10$\frac{1}{2}$" (9cm x 27cm) white cardstock

4" x 4" (10cm x 10cm) medium green cardstock

4$\frac{1}{2}$" x 4$\frac{1}{2}$" (11cm x 11cm) medium yellow cardstock

This card comes courtesy of stamp artist Sandy Sandrus. She has taught this popular folded card many times over the years. It can be adapted to any occasion and is as fun to receive as it is to make. Visualize a photo inside the card when the flaps are opened, or perhaps a small pocket holding a gift certificate or concert tickets!

tip > While these leaf stamps come with their own coordinating veining stamps, if you're using a shadow leaf stamp, you can add your own veining with a gel pen or a fine-point permanent marker. Another option would be to use an embossing pen. This type of pen uses a slow-drying ink which allows you to sprinkle on embossing powder and then heat emboss the image you drew.

one · Place the white cardstock flat on your working surface and stamp solid maple leaves in Peach Pastel ink over the entire top and bottom of the card. Let some of the leaves run off the edges. Repeat with more maple leaves in the Key Lime ink. Fill in the empty spaces with the solid Oak Leaf stamp, using the Ice Jade ink.

two · With the dragonfly side of the Bug Mini Cube, randomly stamp three dragonflies on the panels in the Stream ink. Use the stamp positioner to add the veins to the Key Lime maple leaves and the oak leaves, using the Turquoise Gem ink. Do not add veins to the Peach Pastel maple leaves.

three · Divide the card into three 3½" (9cm) sections by scoring with the bone folder and using the ruler as a guide. Fold the card into thirds along your scored lines. Unfold and then score two more lines on the diagonal on the first and third panels. These diagonal lines must run parallel to each other.

four · Fold one third of the card in and then fold a flap back on the newly-scored diagonal line.

five · Repeat for the last panel, folding the flap in the opposite direction from the first panel's folded flap. Use the $\frac{1}{8}$" (3mm) hole punch to punch a hole near the fold line of each flap, centering the holes.

six · Thread the sheer ribbon from the inside of the card up to the top of the card for each side.

seven · Tie the ribbon in a bow. Place double-stick tape on the back of the folded card and layer it onto the green cardstock. Using additional tape, layer that piece on top of the yellow cardstock.

windy leaves card

MATERIALS

STAMPS

1" x 1" (3cm x 3cm) Design Block, Square and Frame (Just For Fun)

Maple Leaf Silhouette (Just For Fun)

Oak Leaf 1 Silhouette (Just For Fun)

Oak Leaf 2 Silhouette (Just For Fun)

Birch Leaf Silhouette (Just For Fun)

Design Block Mini Cube (Just For Fun)

INK PADS

California Stucco, Antiquities (Ranger)

Rose Quartz, Antiquities (Ranger)

Ochre, Antiquities (Ranger)

Topiary, Antiquities (Ranger)

Chinese Red, Antiquities (Ranger)

Cobalt, Antiquities (Ranger)

OTHER ITEMS

mini zig-zag decorative-edged scissors

double-stick tape

PAPER PREPARATION

2^1/$_4$" x 4^3/$_4$" (8cm x 12cm) white cardstock

2^5/$_8$" x 5^1/$_8$" (7cm x 13cm) dark orange cardstock

2^5/$_8$" x 5^1/$_8$" (7cm x 13cm) coral cardstock

5^1/$_2$" x 8^1/$_2$" (14cm x 22cm) pearlescent peach cardstock

one • With the shadow side of the 1" x 1" (3cm x 3cm) Design Block, stamp a row of squares using the California Stucco, Rose Quartz and Ochre inks on the white cardstock.

two • Stamp a leaf onto each of the squares, alternating between the Topiary and Chinese Red inks. Using the Design Block Mini Cube, stamp the parallel line pattern in Cobalt over each leaf image, alternating the direction of the lines with each leaf.

This card goes together very quickly and uses shadow stamps to create a nice background for the leaves. When stamping with shadow stamps, choose inks that are light in color so that darker images, stamped on top, clearly show.

three • Layer the stamped piece onto the dark orange cardstock and trim closely with the mini zig-zag scissors. Take care to line up the pattern of the scissors with every cut. Fold the pearlescent peach cardstock in half. Using double-stick tape, layer the trimmed piece onto the coral cardstock and then attach to the front of the peach card.

fun circles card

MATERIALS

STAMPS

Design Block Circle and Frame
(Just For Fun)

Graphics Block (Just For Fun)

Bugs Mini Cube (Just For Fun)

Small Script (Just For Fun)

Ladybug Sketch (Just For Fun)

Romantic Charms Mini Cube
(Just For Fun)

INK PADS

Ocean Aqua, Sea Shells (Ranger)

Tropical Raspberry, Sea Shells (Ranger)

Peach Bellini, Sea Shells (Ranger)

Sea Grass, Sea Shells (Ranger)

Conch Shell, Sea Shells (Ranger)

Starfish Green, Sea Shells (Ranger)

Jet Black, Staz-On (Tsukineko)

OTHER ITEMS

large sticky notes

craft knife

cutting mat

PAPER PREPARATION

Six-panel White Luster accordion card
(The Paper Cut)

This project calls for a bit of masking magic—well, not magic really, but the results suggest it! This project leaves plenty of room for variation, and it could be easily adapted to suit a number of different occasions. Arm yourself with a pad of those handy sticky notes.

one · Cut the accordion card apart into three, two-panel cards. Keep one to use for this project and save the other two for future use. Using the six colors of Sea Shells inks and the Design Block Circle stamp, stamp nine solid circles onto the front of the card in a three-by-three row pattern.

two · Stamp the same circle onto a large sticky note (or piece of scrap paper).

three · Cut out the interior of the circle with a craft knife. You've now created a reverse mask! Place the mask over one of the circles and stamp an image over the mask with the black ink. Press firmly to ensure stamping from edge to edge.

four · Add a contrasting color background using the Graphics Block. Because this is a long stamp, use extra sticky notes to cover up areas of your card where you do not want the image stamped. Continue stamping random images and backgrounds over the rest of the circles, using the Bugs Mini Cube, Small Script, Ladybug Sketch and Romantic Charms Mini Cube stamps.

swirl shaker card

MATERIALS

STAMPS

Square Shaker Template (Art Gone Wild!)

Scratchboard Cube (Just For Fun)

Swirl-in-Hand (angi-b & co.)

Swirl Shapes Cube (Alias Smith & Rowe)

INK PADS

Ice Jade, Fluid Chalks, ColorBox
(Clearsnap)

Peach Pastel, Fluid Chalks, ColorBox
(Clearsnap)

French Blue, Fluid Chalks, ColorBox
(Clearsnap)

Rouge, Fluid Chalks, ColorBox (Clearsnap)

Frost White, ColorBox (Clearsnap)

OTHER ITEMS

scissors

bone folder

ruler

craft knife

cutting mat

double-stick tape

foam tape

confetti (or micro beads or glitter)

PAPER PREPARATION

$5^1/_2$" x $8^1/_2$" (14cm x 22cm)
white cardstock

$2^1/_4$" x $2^1/_4$" (6cm x 6cm)
white cardstock

$2^1/_2$" x $2^1/_2$" (6cm x 6cm)
clear acetate

$2^3/_4$" x $2^7/_8$" (7cm x 7cm)
medium yellow cardstock

$5^1/_2$" x $8^1/_2$" (14cm x 22cm)
coral cardstock

Here's a great surprise for a lucky recipient—a color-ful shaker card! And the card is simple to make, thanks to a rubber stamp from Art Gone Wild! that makes the shaker portion as easy as cut, fold and tape. Fill the shaker with a magical mixture of festive tid bits: confetti, beads, tiny buttons, shrink plastic pieces—whatever your imagination dishes out!

one · Stamp the Square Shaker Template stamp on the wrong side of the large piece of white cardstock, using a pale color of ink (such as the Peach Pastel). Cut the template out with scissors and use the bone folder and ruler to score all of the dotted lines. Use the craft knife to cut the window out. Turn the piece over to the right side and stamp with the four colors of chalk inks using the swirl side of the Scratchboard Cube, as shown.

two · Ink up the Swirl-in-Hand stamp with the same four colors of chalk inks, applying the ink by tapping it on, from the corners of the ink pads. Stamp the hand on the small square of white cardstock and use double-stick tape to adhere the piece to one of the short flaps on the window piece.

three · Use double-stick tape to adhere the square of clear acetate to the wrong side of the window opening. Add narrow strips of foam tape on top of the acetate, around the window. Sprinkle confetti (or buttons, beads or glitter) into the cavity.

four · Peel the paper liner off the foam tape and fold the flap with the hand piece over the confetti. Then secure the other short flap on top with double-stick tape. Fold the two long flaps over and secure with more double-stick tape. Layer the shaker piece onto the yellow cardstock and set aside. Fold the Coral cardstock in half. Randomly stamp with the round swirl from the Swirl Shapes cube with the Frost White pigment ink on the front of the coral card. Use double-stick tape to attach the layered shaker piece to the front of the card.

ballerina card

MATERIALS

STAMPS

Degas' Fluffing the Tutu (Just For Fun)

Assorted Motifs Block (Just For Fun)

Background 2 Cube (Just For Fun)

INK PADS

Jet Black, Staz-On (Tsukineko)

Tropical Raspberry, Sea Shells (Ranger)

Cool Peri, Sea Shells (Ranger)

Gold, Encore (Tsukineko)

OTHER ITEMS

stamp positioner (EK Success)

sticky notes

colored pencils
(pinks and purples)

cutting mat

craft knife

stipple brush

24" (61cm) sheer pink ribbon

PAPER PREPARATION

White Luster Double Shutter card
(The Paper Cut)

H ere's another unique fold, incorporated into what's called a Double Shutter card. Wrapped up with a pretty bow, it almost looks like a gift in and of itself!

one · Open the left side of the shutter card. Use the stamp positioner to stamp the ballerina, in Jet Black ink, on the fold.

two · Stamp the ballerina again on a sticky note and set it aside. Color the ballerina on the card with colored pencils. Place the card on a cutting mat and, using a craft knife, cut along the outline of the portion of the ballerina that extends to the right of the fold.

three · Pop out the portion that was cut out and close the left flap. The cutout portion of the ballerina should now extend over the right shutter flap of the card. Cut out the ballerina that was stamped on the sticky note to create a mask. Position the mask on top of the colored ballerina on the closed card. Use the stipple brush and the Tropical Raspberry ink to apply color down the center of the card and around both sides of the ballerina. Remember to stipple ink on the right shutter flap underneath the ballerina as well. Keep the mask in place. Apply the Cool Peri ink on the musical staff from the Assorted Motifs block and stamp it three times in horizontal rows down the front of the card, right on top of the masked ballerina and stippled background.

four · Apply the gold pigment ink to the "flecks" side of the Background 2 Cube and stamp over the entire front of the card, keeping the mask in place. Remove the mask and tie the pink ribbon around the card to finish.

jukebox pop-up card

MATERIALS

STAMPS

Design Block Square and Frame 1" x 1" (3cm x 3cm) (Just For Fun)

Design Block Square and Frame 1³/₄" x 1³/₄" (4cm x 4cm) (Just For Fun)

Torn Paper Design Block, 2-Sided (Just For Fun)

Atom (Just For Fun)

Jukebox (Just For Fun)

45 RPM (Just For Fun)

Record Border (Just For Fun)

INK PADS

Rouge, Fluid Chalks, ColorBox (Clearsnap)

Peach Pastel, Fluid Chalks, ColorBox (Clearsnap)

Ice Jade, Fluid Chalks, ColorBox (Clearsnap)

Turquoise Gem, VersaMagic (Tsukineko)

Jet Black, Staz-On (Tsukineko)

OTHER ITEMS

scissors

clear glitter glue

water-based markers (American Tombow, Inc.)

1³/₄" (4cm) circle punch

1" (3cm) circle punch

plastic palette

blender pen

double-stick tape

foam tape

PAPER PREPARATION

5¹/₄" x 8¹/₄" (13cm x 21cm) glossy white cardstock

3" x 5" (8cm x 13cm) glossy white cardstock

glossy white cardstock scraps

5¹/₂" x 8¹/₂" (14cm x 22cm) bright blue cardstock

1¹/₄" x 5¹/₂" (3cm x 14cm) glossy white cardstock

1¹/₂" x 5¹/₂" (4cm x 14cm) glossy black cardstock

It's time to rock and roll with an easy pop-up card that will bring smiles to the recipient—if you can bear to part with it! There are a few more steps to this card than there are for some of the others, but it's quite easy to assemble. Bright colors guarantee cheerful thoughts.

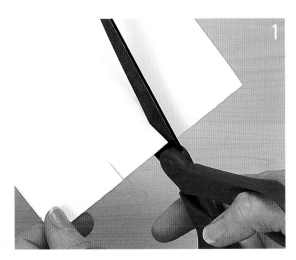

one · Using the shadow side of the two Design Blocks and the smaller square on the Torn Paper Block, use the Rouge, Peach Pastel, Ice Jade and Turquoise Gem ink pads to randomly stamp onto one side of the large glossy white cardstock. Keep the orientation of all the shadow shapes square and straight. Don't be tempted to fill in all of the white space. When dry, randomly stamp approximately nine of the atoms using the Jet Black ink, allowing some to be stamped off the edge of the page. Fold the stamped piece in half and make two $1/2$" (32mm) cuts about $1^3/4$" (4cm) apart in the center of the fold, using scissors.

two · Fold the cut flap back and forth a few times to make it flexible. Open the card and pop the flap out toward you as shown. You've just created the liner for the pop-up card!

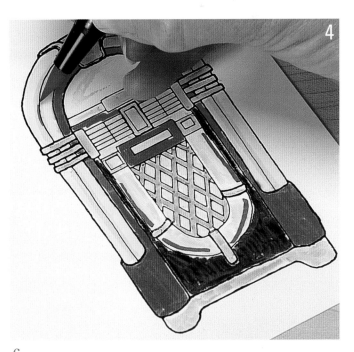

three · Lay the piece flat and apply the glitter glue to the atoms to create sparkle. Let this thoroughly dry.

four · Stamp the jukebox onto the smaller rectangle of glossy cardstock using the Jet Black ink. When the ink is dry, color it in with the markers.

five • Stamp two of the 45 RPM images on a scrap of glossy white cardstock, using the Jet Black ink. When they are dry, punch them out with the 1¾" (4cm) circle punch.

six • Stamp the Record Border onto a scrap of glossy white cardstock using the Jet Black ink. Punch them out with the 1" (3cm) circle punch. Scribble a little color from the markers onto a plastic palette (such as the lid from a margarine tub) and pick up the color with a blender pen. Apply this light shade of ink to the record labels, then outline them with the marker to make a darker border on the label. Color all of the labels in the same manner.

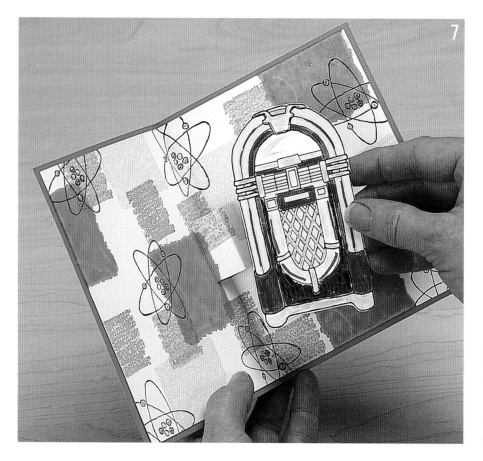

*tip > To create the 45s, if you don't wish to use a circle punch, try using either a circle template and scissors, or a circle template and a shape-cutting system. Shape-cutting systems are available at your local craft or stamp stores.

seven • Cut out the jukebox with scissors, leaving a small border around the outline. Apply double-stick tape to the wrong side of the pop-up liner and adhere it to the inside of the folded blue card. Apply a piece of double-stick tape to the pop-up flap and adhere the jukebox to the flap.

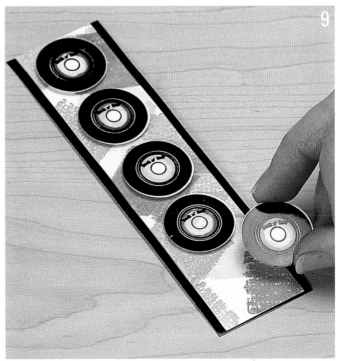

eight · Add a small piece of double-stick tape to the edges of the larger 45s and attach them behind the jukebox, taking care that they don't protrude beyond the edges of the card when it is closed. On the 1¼" x 5½" (3cm x 14cm) of glossy cardstock, stamp the 1" x 1" (3cm x 3cm) Design Block square with the three colors of chalk ink. Vary the direction of the shadow and let the image run off the edges of the cardstock.

nine · Layer the stamped strip onto the glossy black cardstock. Use foam tape to adhere the smaller 45s in a row down the stamped strip.

ten · Place double-stick tape on the back of the glossy black cardstock and attach the strip to the front of the card.

eleven · Apply glitter glue to the tube sections of the jukebox, and you're ready to rock and roll!

leaf pop-up card

MATERIALS

STAMPS

Tumbling Leaves (Alias Smith & Rowe)

Oak Leaf, 2-Sided (Just For Fun)

Maple Leaf, 2-Sided (Just For Fun)

Birch Leaf, 2-Sided (Just For Fun)

"Leaves" (Just For Fun)

INK PADS

Caribbean Sea, Kaleidacolor (Tsukineko)

Lime, ColorBox (Clearsnap)

Bottle, Adirondack (Ranger)

Yellow-Green, Marvy Matchables No. 52 (Uchida)

Stream, Adirondack (Ranger)

Lettuce, Adirondack (Ranger)

Meadow, Adirondack (Ranger)

OTHER ITEMS

sticky notes or scrap paper

stamp positioner (EK Success)

scissors

double-stick tape

deckle-edged scissors

foam tape

PAPER PREPARATION

White Luster Finger Card Kit (The Paper Cut)

white cardstock scraps for leaves

$3^{1}/_{4}$" x $4^{1}/_{2}$" (8cm x 11cm) white cardstock

$4^{1}/_{4}$" x $5^{1}/_{2}$" (11cm x 14cm) teal cardstock

$3^{3}/_{4}$" x 5" (10cm x 13cm) yellow-orange cardstock

$1^{1}/_{2}$" x 3" (4cm x 8cm) teal cardstock

Can you tell I'm partial to leaves? At first glance, you may think "Oh no, this is *way* too complicated!" But it's not! With a prescored finger card kit, you can create this card easily and with little effort. But you don't have to let the recipient of the card know that!

one · Open up the card so that the half with three scored lines close together is on your right. Position a large sticky note or scrap paper to the left of the center score line so that the left side is masked. Using the Caribbean Sea rainbow pad and the Tumbling Leaves stamp, randomly stamp and fill the entire surface of the card to the right of the masked area.

two · Using the two-sided leaf stamps and the stamp positioner, stamp onto white cardstock scraps, two oak leaves in Lime and their veins in Bottle. Stamp two maple leaves in Yellow-Green and their veins in Stream. Stamp two more maple leaves in Lettuce and their veins in Stream. Stamp four birch leaves in Meadow and their veins in Bottle. Set these stamped leaves aside.

three · Ink up the oak leaf with Lime, then pat the edges of the leaf with Stream. This is going to be the leaf for the cover of the card.

four · Stamp this oak leaf once onto another scrap of white cardstock and stamp its veins with Bottle, again, using the stamp positioner. On the 3¹/₄" x 4¹/₂" (8cm x 11cm) piece of white cardstock, stamp more Tumbling Leaves with the Caribbean Sea rainbow pad, completely covering the piece. Cut out all of the two-sided leaves from step two and the cover leaf from step three, leaving a small border around each.

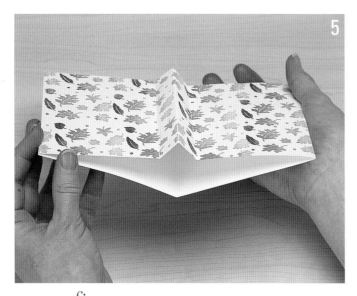

five · Prefold the score lines on the card, creating a mountain fold for the center of the group of three scored lines and a valley fold on either side of it. Apply double-stick tape to the back of the stamped section, avoiding the group of three folds. Line up the two outside edges and secure.

six · Set aside three of the finger strips from the card kit. Use Bottle ink to stamp the word *leaves* on one of the strips. With small pieces of double-stick tape, attach three leaves to the front of each strip and one to the back. On the *leaves* strip, attach one leaf to the front and two or three to the back.

seven · Using double-stick tape, adhere the three finger strips to the inside of the card, on the mountain fold. Alternate the direction of each one.

eight · Adhere the Tumbling Leaves cardstock piece to the 4¼" x 5½" (11cm x 14cm) piece of teal cardstock with double-stick tape and trim closely with the deckle-edged scissors. Layer the trimmed piece onto the yellow-orange cardstock and then layer all pieces to the front of the card. Adhere the remaining oak leaf to the smaller piece of teal cardstock with foam tape and layer this to the front of the card with double-stick tape.

scrapbook page

MATERIALS

STAMPS

Birch Leaf, 2-Sided (Just For Fun)

Oak Leaf, 2-Sided (Just For Fun)

Maple Leaf, 2-Sided (Just For Fun)

INK PADS

Moss Green, ColorBox (Clearsnap)

Roussillon, ColorBox (Clearsnap)

Amber, ColorBox (Clearsnap)

Alpine, ColorBox (Clearsnap)

Merlot, ColorBox (Clearsnap)

OTHER ITEMS

stamp positioner (EK Success)

scissors

foam tape

glue dots

photo

clear archival photo corners (Xyron)

double-stick tape

self-adhesive letters (Life's Journey)

PAPER PREPARATION

12" x 12" (30cm x 30cm) butterscotch cardstock

scraps of butterscotch cardstock

12" x 12" (30cm x 30cm) sage green cardstock

deep red and teal cardstocks for layering your photo

one · Create a path of leaves running diagonally across the butterscotch page using Moss Green for the birch leaves, Roussillon for the oak leaves and Amber for the maple leaves. Use the stamp positioner to stamp the birch veins in Alpine, the oak veins in Merlot and the maple veins in Roussillon.

two · Stamp four more of each leaf and veining onto the butterscotch scraps, using the same colors as before and cut them all out. Tear two opposite corners from the sage green cardstock and mount them in the two opposite corners of the stamped butterscotch page. Apply foam tape to the backs of some of the leaves and glue dots to the rest and mount them over the two sage corners, leaving room for your photo.

Yes, more leaves. And yes, you can stamp in your scrapbook! With the wide range of acid-free inks, papers and adhesives, there's no limit to your creativity.

three · Mount your photo onto the red cardstock using the archival photo corners, then layer the red cardstock onto the teal using double-stick tape. Mount the layered photo onto the center of the page with double-stick tape. Use self-adhesive letters to create a title and place it below the photo.

special occasions

This chapter features many different ideas for all those special occasions in your life. From birthdays to get-wells and thank-yous to winter time holidays, you'll find plenty of inspiration to get your creative juices flowing and to start celebrating!

But don't stop there! Though the ideas and images here are designed for specific themes, there's no reason why you can't take one of these ideas and adapt it to your own special occasion. Rubber stamping is nothing if not versatile!

By using colors that are bright and cheerful, your cards will become true gifts for the recipients. Simplicity is the key here, and each of these cards is easy to put together. That can be a real lifesaver when time is of the essence.

CHAPTER

birthday cake card

MATERIALS

STAMPS

Birthday Frame (Just For Fun)

Cake with Candles, Small (Just For Fun)

Graphics Block (Just For Fun)

INK PADS

Clear Embossing, Top Boss (Clearsnap)

Harmony Pastel (Tsukineko)

Stream, Adirondack (Ranger)

OTHER

stamp positioner (EK Success)

gold embossing powder

heat gun

waterbrush or watercolor brush

watercolor paints

deckle-edged scissors

double-stick tape

PAPER PREPARATION

3^1/$_8$" x 3^1/$_8$" (8cm x 8cm)
white cardstock

3^3/$_4$" x 5" (10cm x 13cm)
white cardstock

3^1/$_8$" x 3^1/$_8$" (8cm x 8cm)
lavender cardstock

5^1/$_2$" x 8^1/$_2$" (14cm x 22cm)
lavender cardstock

Here's a fanciful card that conjures up visions of a party! The four-sided Birthday Frame features a blank center that can have either an image stamped in it or a shape punched out of it. A stamp positioner will help with exact placement of the images.

tip > Any pigment ink pad can be used in place of an embossing pad, if you're in a pinch. Although it's not mandatory, it's a good idea to use a pigment color that is close to the color of your embossing powder.

one · Stamp the Birthday Frame onto the stamp positioner's imaging plate, using any nonpermanent dye-based ink.

two · Place the stamped imaging plate on top of the white cardstock square and move it about until you see that the stamped image is centrally located. Place the stamp positioner handle back in place and hold it securely.

three · Remove the imaging plate. Stamp the image directly onto the cardstock with embossing ink while continuing to hold the handle in place.

4

tip > For embossing powders that you use frequently, a plastic food storage container works wonderfully for storage and it doubles as a place to tap off excess powder. Funneling the extra powder back into the container is also much easier than getting it back into a small jar.

four · Sprinkle gold embossing powder over the wet ink and tap off the excess.

5

6

7

five · Heat to melt the powder.

six · Stamp the Cake with Candles onto the center and emboss with gold powder just like you did for the Birthday Frame.

seven · Using the swirl side of the Graphics Block, use the Harmony Pastel rainbow ink pad to diagonally stamp the swirls onto the larger white cardstock.

eight · Paint the birthday cake with water-color paints using the waterbrush. Keep the application of color light—you won't need much paint.

nine · Trim the cake piece with deckle-edged scissors and use double-stick tape to layer it onto the square piece of lavender cardstock. Adhere this layered piece to the center of the swirled background. Fold the larger piece of lavender cardstock in half. Apply double-stick tape to the back of the background piece and attach it to the front of the lavender card.

ANOTHER SIMPLY
BEAUTIFUL
IDEA

The Birthday Cake card was taken a step further by stamping brush marks on a square of white cardstock with some soft ink colors. A square punch was used to remove the center from the stamped square, and a stamp positioner helped to align and stamp the Birthday Frame. The Cake with Candles was stamped, colored and cut out, then foam-taped in the center of the frame. Another layer of cardstock was added and trimmed with scalloped-edged scissors. The frame was attached to a card that had been stamped with an interesting texture.

cherry blossom card

MATERIALS

STAMPS

Cherry Blossom Branch (Just For Fun)

Double Happy Birthday (Just For Fun)

INK PADS

Clear Embossing, Top Boss (Clearsnap)

OTHER ITEMS

copper embossing powder

heat gun

ruler

scallop-edged scissors

waterbrush

Pearl Ex Interference watercolors: Pearl White, Interference Red, Interference Blue, Interference Green

Twinkling H20's paint (LuminArte): Indian Copper

double-stick tape

PAPER PREPARATION

8¼" x 8½" (21cm x 22cm) moss green cardstock

4" x 8½" (10cm x 22cm) handmade decorative paper

This birthday card is sophisticated in appearance and mood. A simple cut with decorative-edged scissors makes it unique! We add sparkle with the addition of iridescent paints made from mica-based pigment powders. These glimmering paints are water-based and are applied just like any other watercolors.

one · Fold the moss green cardstock in half lengthwise and stamp with the Cherry Blossom Branch using embossing ink. Stamp the branch about three times, positioning it off the edges of the card. Sprinkle copper embossing powder over all and heat with the heat gun to melt the powder. You may stamp and emboss one image at a time if it's easier. Stamp the Double Happy Birthday with embossing ink in the approximate center, keeping the phrase closer to the folded edge of the card. Heat emboss with the copper embossing powder as you did before.

two · Measure in approximately 1¾" (4cm) from the bottom outside edge of the card and begin cutting with the scallop-edged scissors, forming a curve from the mark to the top left corner.

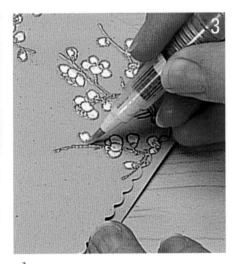

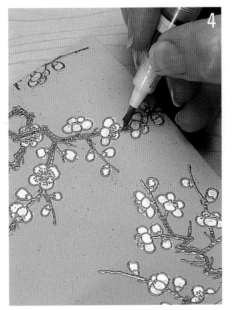

three · Using the water brush and the Pearl Ex watercolors, begin painting in the blossoms on the branches. Apply the Pearl White to each blossom first and allow it to dry. Add touches of the Interference Red to the blossoms and just a few dots of the Interference Blue to suggest subtle shading.

four · Add a spot of Interference Green at the base of each blossom where it connects to the branch. Fill in the branches with the Indian Copper.

five · Open the card and attach the piece of decorative paper to the inside, using double-stick tape. This acts as a nice liner on which to write.

three gifts card

MATERIALS

STAMPS

Gift Cube (Just For Fun)

INK PADS

Jet Black, Staz-On (Tsukineko)

OTHER ITEMS

colored pencils

double-stick tape

foam tape

PAPER PREPARATION

1⁵/₈" x 2" (4cm x5cm)
white cardstock, 3 pieces

1⁷/₈" x 4" (5cm x 10cm)
bright yellow cardstock

1⁷/₈" x 4" (5cm x 10cm)
bright blue cardstock

1⁷/₈" x 4" (5cm x 10cm)
bright red cardstock

8" x 8¹/₂" (20cm x 22cm)
ribbed white cardstock

Here is another very easy and quick-to-put-together card, perfect for a birthday celebration. Textured white cardstock adds an extra dimension and contrasts nicely with the bright colors of the layers. Torn paper edges make it artsy!

one · Stamp three of the four packages from the Gift Cube onto the three pieces of white cardstock, using the Jet Black ink pad. Color in the images with colored pencils, using a separate color for each of the boxes and separate contrasting colors for each of the bows.

two · Use double-stick tape to attach each of the gifts to the brightly colored cardstock pieces so that the border on the top and sides are even and there is a bit more border at the bottom. Tear along this bottom edge. Don't worry about the torn edges being even; the irregularities are desirable!

three · Apply foam tape to the back of the colored cardstock pieces.

four · After folding the ribbed cardstock piece in half to make an 8¹/₂" x 4" (22cm x 10cm) card, position the pieces onto the card, evenly spacing them. Adhere them in a horizontal row, to the front of the card.

thank-you card

MATERIALS

STAMPS

Torn Paper Design Block, 2-Sided
(Just For Fun)

Thank You Word Frame (Just For Fun)

Background Cube (Just For Fun)

Dandelion, Small (Just For Fun)

Butterfly (Inky Antics)

INK PADS

Ochre, Antiquities (Ranger)

French Blue, ColorBox (Clearsnap)

Spring Pansy, VersaMagic (Tsukineko)

Jet Black, Staz-On (Tsukineko)

OTHER ITEMS

sticky notes or scrap paper

stamp positioner (EK Success)

waterbrush

Twinkling H2O's: Sunflower,
Sky Blue, Bougainvillea

PAPER PREPARATION

White Luster Tri-fold Window Card
(The Paper Cut)

This card features another special die-cut—one that folds into a Z formation and has two windows. Repeated stamping from a cube stamp creates a background that suggests a textured surface. While your sentiment might be "thank-you," it's the recipient that will be giving the thanks for this special card.

one · Open the card and lay it flat so that the larger window is on your right. Place a piece of scrap paper under the small window in the center panel so that your work surface is protected. Ink up the larger shadow square on the Torn Paper Design Block with the Ochre ink and use the stamp positioner to stamp it over the smaller window. Stamp the Thank You Word Frame over the Ochre shadow in French Blue, again using the stamp positioner.

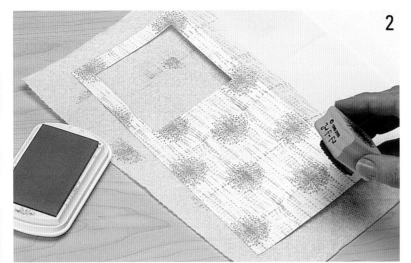

two · Turn the card over so that the large window is now on your left. Place sticky notes or scrap paper to the right of the first fold line to protect the center panel. With the gauze side of the Background Cube, stamp in Spring Pansy over the entire surface of the large window panel. With the Dandelion stamp and French Blue ink, stamp a pattern of dandelions over the gauzy texture.

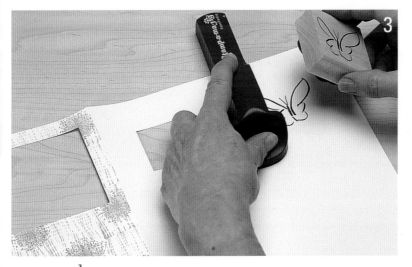

three · Close up the card and lay it face up on the table. Stamp the butterfly on the stamp positioner's imaging plate and slip the plate underneath the Z-fold and against the back panel of the card so that you can see the butterfly through both windows. Hold the plate securely while you carefully open up the card as shown above. Use the stamp positioner to stamp the butterfly in place, using Jet Black ink.

four · Paint the butterfly with the Twinkling H2O's, using the waterbrush.

get well card

MATERIALS

STAMPS

Large Star, Ragged (Alias Smith & Rowe)

Heart Person (angi-b & co.)

Jumping Dancer Solid (angi-b & co.)

Magic Wand (angi-b & co.)

Swirl Shapes Cube (Alias Smith & Rowe)

INK PADS

Bouquet, Kaleidacolor (Tsukineko)

Yellow, Marvy Matchable No. 5 (Uchida)

Light Blue, Marvy Matchable No. 10 (Uchida)

PAPER PREPARATION

White Luster six-panel accordion card (The Paper Cut)

Now here's a card to raise someone's spirits! A colorful dancer cartwheels across the panels of an accordion card to bring happy greetings and lots of good cheer.

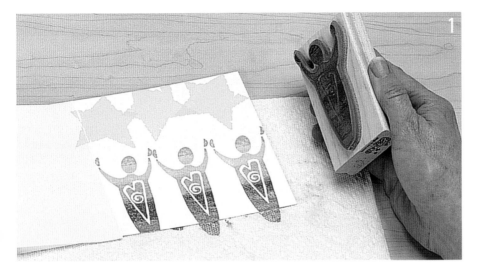

one · On the accordion's front panel, stamp three stars in yellow ink across the top. Stamp the Heart Person three times across the bottom using the Bouquet rainbow pad.

two · Turn the card over and lay it out flat. Ink up the Jumping Dancer with the Bouquet pad, applying in stages so the entire rubber die has been inked (the rubber die is slightly longer than the rainbow ink pad). Stamp the first image in the first panel so that it appears to be entering the card from the lower left corner, running the stamp off the page. Continue stamping the Jumping Dancer with the same ink, positioning it so that you create the look of an ongoing cartwheel across all six panels. Have the figure run off the last panel.

*tip > When working with rainbow pads, take care not to drag or rub the stamp across the pad so you don't contaminate one color with another.

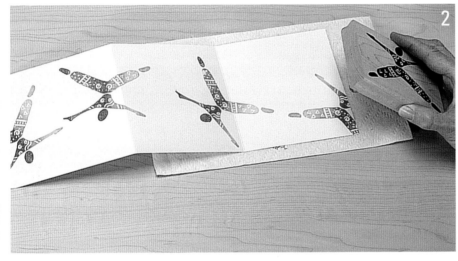

three · With the yellow ink pad and the star stamp, stamp one star somewhere between each of the figures to act as a visual connector. Stamp the Magic Wand in the Light Blue ink along the top and bottom length of the card.

four · Using the round swirl and the square swirl from the Swirl Shapes Cube, randomly add swirls to the card, picking up individual colors from the Bouquet rainbow pad.

valentine swirl card

MATERIALS

STAMPS

Scratchboard Cube (Just For Fun)

Mini Design Block Cube (Just For Fun)

Heart Cube (Just For Fun)

INK PADS

Pink Pizazz, Ancient Page (Clearsnap)

Flamingo, Ancient Page (Clearsnap)

OTHER ITEMS

scissors

foam tape

double-stick tape

scallop-edged decorative scissors

PAPER PREPARATION

3½" x 4¾" (9cm x 12cm)
white cardstock

2½" x 2½" (6cm x 6cm)
white cardstock, 3 pieces

4" x 5½" (10cm x 14cm)
dark fuschia cardstock

5½" x 8½" (14cm x 22cm)
pink cardstock

Shadow-style stamping creates a contemporary-looking Valentine card for your sweetheart. Don't forget to add a personal note inside!

one · Stamp two squares from the swirl side of the Scratch-board Cube onto the large white cardstock using Pink Pizazz ink.

two · Add smaller squares with the Mini Design Block Cube, filling in around the first two swirl squares with the Flamingo ink. Don't worry about perfect placement; visible gaps will get covered up with hearts.

three · On the small squares of white card-stock, stamp two hearts from the Heart Cube with Flamingo ink and another heart with Pink Pizazz.

four · Cut out the hearts, leaving a small border around each one. Add foam tape pieces to the backs of the hearts and layer them onto the stamped cardstock. Layer the stamped piece onto the dark fuschia cardstock with double-stick tape and trim closely with the scallop-edged scissors. Fold the pink cardstock in half, then, use double-stick tape to layer the heart piece onto the pink card.

mother's day card

MATERIALS

STAMPS

Faux Post Cube (Just For Fun)

Faux Post Cube Template (Just For Fun)

Long Stem Rose (Just For Fun)

Background Block (Just For Fun)

INK PADS

Jet Black, Staz-On (Tsukineko)

Tropical Raspberry, Sea Shells (Ranger)

Gold, Encore (Tsukineko)

OTHER ITEMS

bone folder

ruler

stipple brushes

colored pencils: pink and green

stamp-edged decorative scissors (Fiskars)

double-stick tape

PAPER PREPARATION

5$\frac{1}{2}$" x 8$\frac{1}{2}$" (14cm x 22cm)
pink cardstock

white cardstock scraps
(for faux post image)

1$\frac{1}{2}$" x 2" (4cm x 5cm)
sage green cardstock

2" x 2" (5cm x 5cm)
sage green cardstock

Send a Mother's Day card with lovely rose faux post stamps on the front of this easy tri-fold shutter card. Consider placing a photo inside!

one · Use the bone folder and ruler to score and fold a line 2⅛" (5cm) from each end of the pink cardstock to form a shutter card. Using the Faux Post Cube, stamp one square and one rectangle on the white cardstock scraps using the Jet Black ink. Using the template made for the cube to mask out the dotted lines, stipple Tropical Raspberry ink over the surface of each shape. Stipple with the gold ink around the edges of each shape. Stamp the Long Stem Rose in Jet Black over the stippling on each faux post. Remove the template and color the roses in with colored pencils.

two · Cut out both of the faux post with the stamp-edged decorative scissors, leaving about ⅛" (3mm) border around the dotted lines. Using double-stick tape, adhere the pieces to the small pieces of sage green cardstock.

three · Make sure both shutter flaps of the card are closed. Stamp the script side of the Background Block in Tropical Raspberry three times horizontally down the front of the card.

four · Adhere the faux postage pieces to the front of the card with double-stick tape, attaching one to each shutter flap. Place the square piece on the upper left half and the rectangle on the lower right half. Each faux post will overlap on the opposite flap.

father's day card

MATERIALS

STAMPS

Watch Profile (Just For Fun)

Watch Face, Large (Just For Fun)

Tiny Pocketwatch (Just For Fun)

Multi-Faced Watch (Just For Fun)

Background Cube (Just For Fun)

INK PADS

Stonewashed, Adirondack (Ranger)

Wild Plum, Adirondack (Ranger)

Jet Black, Staz-On (Tsukineko)

Clear Embossing, Top Boss (Clearsnap)

OTHER ITEMS

stipple brushes

paper towel

silver embossing powder

heat gun

silver leafing pen (Krylon)

double-stick tape

PAPER PREPARATION

3$^1/_4$" x 4" (8cm x 10cm)
white cardstock

3$^5/_8$" x 4$^3/_8$" (9cm x 11cm)
reddish purple cardstock

5$^1/_2$" x 8$^1/_2$" (14cm x 22cm)
light blue cardstock

Don't be stumped about what to stamp for the men in your life. Masculine colors and "manly" images abound in the rubber stamp world. This card features numerous time pieces in a rubber stamped collage.

one · Stipple the Stonewashed and Wild Plum inks sparingly around the perimeter of the white cardstock. Because these are intense colors, it's important to tap off ink onto a paper towel or scrap paper before stippling on the cardstock.

two · Randomly stamp all the clock and watch stamps with the Jet Black ink over the stippled piece. After the black ink has dried, stamp with the circles side of the Background Cube using embossing ink over all the clock images. Sprinkle silver embossing powder over all, tap off the excess and melt with the heat gun.

three · Gild the edge of the finished stamped piece with the silver leafing pen.

four · Fold the light blue cardstock in half. With double-stick tape, layer the stamped piece onto the purple cardstock, then again onto the front of the folded blue card.

back-to-school frame

MATERIALS

STAMPS

Mini Design Block Cube (Just For Fun)

Classic Daisy (Just For Fun)

INK PADS

Verdigris, Antiquities (Ranger)

Bottle, Adirondack (Ranger)

Frost White, ColorBox (Clearsnap)

OTHER ITEMS

clear glitter glue

photo

archival photo corners

double-stick tape

PAPER PREPARATION

Oval Die-Cut overlay card (The Paper Cut)

When the kids bring those school portraits home, send them to the relatives with these quick-to-stamp overlay cards and matching envelopes!

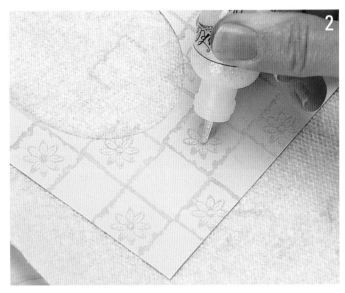

one · Use the Verdigris ink pad to stamp the open frame side of the Mini Design Block Cube in a checkerboard pattern onto the overlay cardstock.

two · Stamp the Classic Daisy in every other frame with the Verdigris ink. Add just a dot of glitter glue in the center of each flower. Let the glitter glue thoroughly dry.

three · Attach your photo to the back of the front panel of the card with the archival photo corners so that it may be seen through the oval window. Decorate the matching envelope by stamping the Classic Daisy with the Bottle and Frost White inks. Leave an open area in the center of the envelope for the address.

four · Apply double-stick tape to the back of the overlay, including around the oval window and center it over the front of the card to adhere it.

spider explosion card

MATERIALS

STAMPS

Spider (Just For Fun)

Big Frank Torso (Just For Fun)

Web Corner (Just For Fun)

"Happy Halloween" (Just For Fun)

Web Background (Just For Fun)

INK PADS

Jet Black, Staz-On (Tsukineko)

Orange, Marvy Matchable No. 7 (Uchida)

OTHER ITEMS

colored pencils

stamp positioner (EK Success)

double-stick tape

zig-zag decorative-edged scissors
(Fiskars)

PAPER PREPARATION

2 1/2" x 1 1/8" (6cm x 3cm)
glossy white cardstock

8" (20cm) square
white text weight paper

5 1/2" x 8 1/2" (14cm x 22cm)
bright orange cardstock

2 1/8" x 3" (5cm x 8cm)
bright orange cardstock

2 1/8" x 3" (5cm x 8cm)
glossy black cardstock

An explosion for Halloween? Well, not really. But you could make this card really "erupt" by filling the inside with Halloween-style confetti before sliding it into an envelope!

one · Stamp the spider onto the piece of glossy white cardstock with the Jet Black ink and set it aside. Position the square of text-weight paper so that it is like a diamond, and using Jet Black ink, stamp Big Frank in the center. Color Frank in with colored pencils.

tip > Because glossy cardstock is less porous than uncoated cardstock, pigment inks can fail to dry properly. To avoid this frustration, add a clear or colored embossing powder to your stamped image and emboss it with a heat gun.

two · Use the stamp positioner and the Jet Black ink to stamp the Web Corner into each of the four corners of the paper, then stamp more Web Corners to fill in around the edges. Turn the stamp in different directions for the webbing to appear more random.

three · Add a spider in each corner with more Jet Black ink. Ink up the *Happy Halloween* stamp with the orange ink pad and then touch the top and bottom edges of the rubber die with black ink. Stamp the words wherever they fit best. When all ink has dried, fold the paper in half lengthwise with the artwork on the outside, and unfold. Then repeat in the opposite direction.

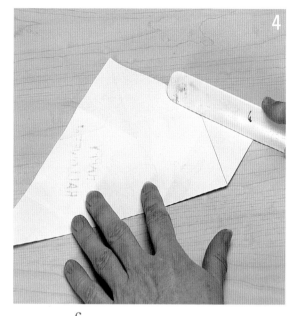

four · Fold the paper in half diagonally, with the artwork on the inside to make a triangle shape. Fold the two corners up toward the top point of the triangle. The tip should not extend more than a touch above the horizontal fold line.

five · Unfold the corners and push them inward and crease.

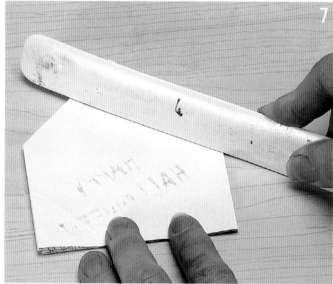

six · Unfold and repeat these diagonal folds in the opposite direction. Now, with all four corners folded inward, collapse the piece.

seven · When pressed flat, the piece should resemble a house.

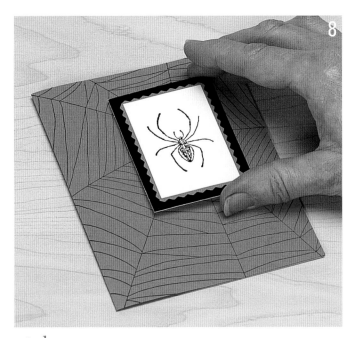

eight · Fold the larger piece of bright orange cardstock in half, and stamp the Web Background onto the front of the orange card with Jet Black ink. This is a very large stamp and will cover the entire front of the card. Mount the spider piece onto the small piece of orange cardstock with double-stick tape and trim closely with the zig-zag scissors. Mount the trimmed piece onto the shiny black cardstock and then layer all on the front of the card.

nine · Apply double-stick tape to one of the house-shaped sides of the folded paper. Adhere it to one side of the inside of the card (be sure the "Happy Halloween" is right-side up). Apply more tape to the other house-shaped side and close the card to secure it in place.

ANOTHER SIMPLY BEAUTIFUL IDEA

This intense explosion results from using a square of spring green text-weight paper and includes a square of white text-weight paper as a layer in the center. Ferns were stamped in the corners and daisies along each edge of the green paper. A touch of white acrylic paint was added to brighten the daisies and make them pop out. The square of white paper was stamped with the border and "Happy Spring," was taped on top of the green paper. All were folded as directed in the Spider Explosion Card.

hanukkah card

MATERIALS

STAMPS

Round Menorah (Ruth's Jewish Stamps)

Jewish Border (Ruth's Jewish Stamps)

Background Cube (Just For Fun)

INK PADS

Clear Embossing, Top Boss (Clearsnap)

OTHER ITEMS

silver embossing powder

heat gun

deckle-edged scissors

foam tape

double-stick tape

PAPER PREPARATION

2¼" x 2¼" (6cm x 6cm)
bright blue cardstock

1½" x 5¼" (4cm x 13cm)
bright blue cardstock

1¼" x 5½" (3cm x 14cm)
silver metallic cardstock

2⅜" x 2½" (6cm x 6cm)
silver metallic cardstock

5½" x 8½" (14cm x 22cm)
bright blue cardstock

Holiday time always seems to sneak up on us every year and we often wonder how to find the time to make handstamped greeting cards. The answer is to keep it simply beautiful! We'll start with a Hanukkah Card that has minimal steps and maximum impact.

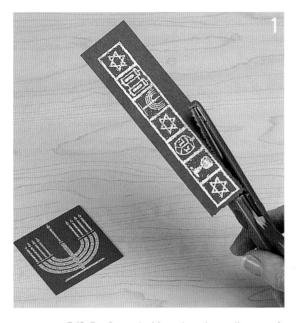

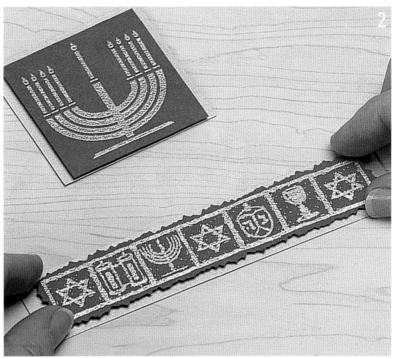

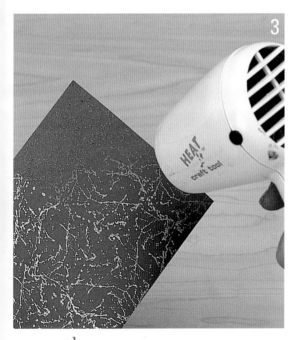

one · Stamp the Menorah on the small square of bright blue cardstock with embossing ink. Sprinkle on silver embossing powder and melt with the heat gun. Stamp the Jewish Border with embossing ink on the long strip of bright blue cardstock and repeat with the silver embossing powder. Trim the border piece with the deckle-edged scissors.

two · Mount each of the embossed pieces onto their corresponding silver pieces of cardstock, using foam tape. The bottom edge of the Menorah piece should be flush with the bottom edge of the silver cardstock.

three · Fold the large piece of bright blue cardstock in half. Use embossing ink to stamp the webbing spray side of the Background Cube onto the front of the folded card and emboss with the silver embossing powder. Continue until the entire front panel of the card is covered with the webbing.

four · Use double-stick tape to mount the border piece along the bottom half of the card. Use double-stick tape to adhere the Menorah at the top of the border as shown so that the bottom edge sits flush against the top of the silver cardstock layer.

poinsettia card

MATERIALS

STAMPS
Poinsettia Sketch (Just For Fun)

"Happy Holidays" (Just For Fun)

INK PADS
Clear Embossing, Top Boss (Clearsnap)

OTHER ITEMS
gold embossing powder

heat gun

waterbrush

watercolor paints (red and green)

scissors

craft knife

cutting mat

foam tape

double-stick tape

PAPER PREPARATION
watercolor paper

3½" x 3¾" (9cm x10cm)
gold cardstock

4" x 5¼" (10cm x 13cm)
red cardstock

5½" x 8½" (14cm x 22cm)
gold cardstock

Many images lend themselves to dimensional layering, such as this poinsettia. By stamping it twice and layering it on top of itself, you can create a very impressive card!

one · Stamp the Poinsettia Sketch twice onto watercolor paper using embossing ink. Emboss with gold embossing powder. With the waterbrush, paint one of the poinsettias with red watercolor and the other with green.

two · When the paint is dry, cut the poinsettias out with scissors, leaving a slight border. Use a craft knife and cutting mat to cut out some of the finer details on the center of the red portion.

three · Apply foam tape to the back of the red poinsettia and adhere it to the green poinsettia, positioning it so green leaves are peeking through the red flowers. Layer the finished poinsettia onto the gold cardstock using double-stick tape.

four · Using embossing ink, stamp *Happy Holidays* onto the bottom of the red cardstock and emboss with the gold embossing powder, using the heat gun.

five · Use double-stick tape to adhere the layered poinsettia piece onto the top of the red cardstock. Fold the larger piece of gold cardstock in half. Adhere the poinsettia piece to the front of the gold card with more double-stick tape.

joy card

MATERIALS

STAMPS

"Joy" (Just For Fun)

Snowflake (Just For Fun)

Large Snowflake (Just For Fun)

INK PADS

Clear Embossing, Top Boss (Clearsnap)

OTHER ITEMS

white embossing powder with
iridescent glitter

heat gun

double-stick tape

ruler

bone folder

PAPER PREPARATION

5¹/₂" x 8¹/₂" (14cm x 22cm)
bright blue cardstock

2¹/₄" x 2¹/₄" (6cm x 6cm)
bright blue cardstock

2³/₈" x 3" (6cm x 8cm)
glossy white cardstock

There's nothing like snowflakes to usher in the Christmas season! This card features an interesting flap on the front that highlights the large snowflake focal point. The bright blue color of the cardstock suggests the chill of a winter's day!

one · Fold the larger piece of bright blue cardstock in half. Ink up the "Joy" stamp with embossing ink and stamp it onto the top right area of the folded card. Sprinkle the glittery white embossing powder over the image, tap off the excess and melt with the heat gun.

two · Randomly stamp the small snowflake with embossing ink over the front of the card. Emboss again with the glittery embossing powder.

three · Stamp the large snowflake on the small square of blue cardstock, using embossing ink, and emboss with the glittery white powder. Use double-stick tape to adhere it to the glossy white cardstock, centering it on one end. Using a ruler as a guide, score a line on the white cardstock with the bone folder, leaving an even border of white all around the blue piece.

four · Place double-stick tape along the back side of the scored section and adhere it to the lower half of the back panel of the card.

great gifts

H ow many times have you found yourself in
a fancy gift shop, looking over the selection
of merchandise and thinking, "I wonder if
I could make that myself?" This chapter shows you
that you can! The following projects are all doable by
anyone who's ever wielded a rubber stamp or two, and
they also emphasize the fact that stamping is a very
versatile hobby.

Of course, it goes without saying (but
I'll say it anyway) that handmade gifts are
the ones that are truly treasured by the
recipients. As gift-giving occasions arise,

you'll look forward to using your rubber
stamps to create gifts and gift containers
that are simply beautiful!

CHAPTER

pearlescent purse

MATERIALS

STAMPS

Purse Template (Alias Smith & Rowe)

Floral Block (Just For Fun)

INK PADS

light-colored dye ink

Clear Embossing, Top Boss (Clearsnap)

OTHER ITEMS

scissors

craft knife

cutting mat

ruler

bone folder

$1/8$" (3mm) hole punch

white embossing powder

heat gun

double-stick tape

gold leafing pen

sheer pink ribbon, 20" (51cm)

PAPER PREPARATION

$5^1/2$" x $8^1/2$" (14cm x 22cm)
pearlescent pink cardstock

Yes, you can stamp a purse! With this wonderful template stamp, you can stamp a bunch of these cute purses and use them as place holders for a party or to stow little treasures for party favors. Imagine presenting one to a special little girl on her birthday!

ANOTHER SIMPLY BEAUTIFUL IDEA

Add whimsy with bright colors and achieve a whole new look. You'll have to find shoes to match, of course!

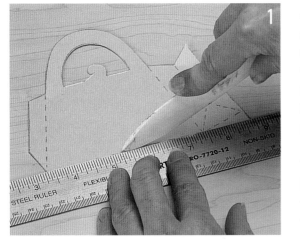

one · Stamp the Purse Template twice on the "wrong" side of the pink cardstock (if there is a "wrong" side). Use the light-colored ink, as you won't want this stamped image to show. Cut out both purse pieces on the solid lines. With the craft knife and a cutting mat, cut out the inside area of the handle. Using the ruler as a guide, score on the dotted lines with the bone folder. Punch holes where you see the dots at the base of the handles (there will be four punched holes) using the 1/8" (3mm) hole punch.

two · Turn the purse pieces over to the "right" side and use embossing ink to horizontally stamp on them with the flower border side of the Floral Block. Stamp the border on the larger side flap of the purse as well, matching the border line from the front and back panels. Emboss with white embossing powder.

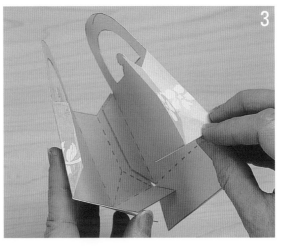

three · Fold along all of the scored lines. Apply double-stick tape to the narrow side flap on both purse halves. Adhere the taped flap of one piece to the wide flap of the other piece. Repeat for the other two flaps.

four · Fold in the small side flaps at the bottom of the purse and put pieces of double-stick tape on them. Adhere one of the large bottom flaps to the tape. Place more double-stick tape on the large bottom flap and fold the final flap over onto it. Use the gold leafing pen to color in the purse clasp at the top.

five · Thread the ribbon through the punched holes and tie a beautiful bow in the front.

terra cotta pot

MATERIALS

STAMPS

Flower (Rubber Stampede)

OTHER ITEMS

terra cotta pot,
3–4" (8cm–10cm) tall, with saucer

foam brush

acrylic paints (Delta Ceramcoat):
Buttercream, Hydrangea Pink, Magenta

cut-up sponge pieces

paper towels

Small terra cotta flower pots are readily available at many craft and garden shops, and you'll find that they're easy and fun to decorate. Foam stamps make it simple to stamp against a less-than-flat surface. These pots can be used as pen/pencil holders, candy-filled party favors or even to plant a flower!

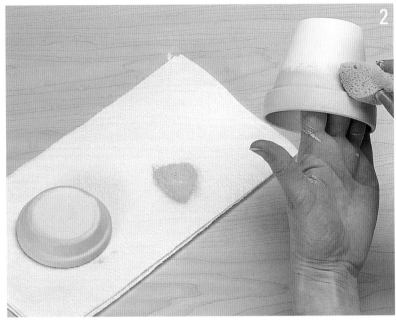

one · Paint at least two coats of the Butter-cream acrylic paint on the entire surface of the pot and saucer, using the foam brush. Let the first coat dry before applying the second coat.

two · Squeeze some of the Hydrangea Pink onto a sponge piece and dab the excess paint on a folded over paper towel. Lightly sponge the paint onto the outside of the saucer and the outside rim of the pot. Let the pink extend slightly beyond the rim of the pot and down the side.

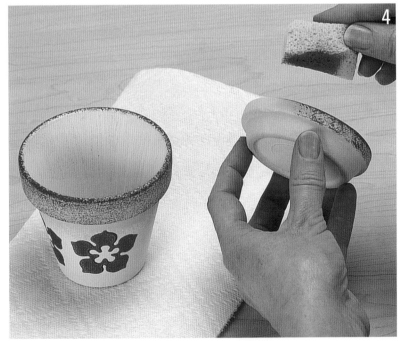

three · After the paint has dried, lightly sponge the Magenta paint onto the foam flower stamp. Place the stamp on the table, die side up. Roll the pot over the stamp to apply the image. Repeat until you have about four flowers stamped around the perimeter of the pot.

four · Using the same sponge you used in step three, lightly sponge the Magenta paint around the outside of the rim of the pot and around the outside of the rim of the saucer.

mini journal

MATERIALS

STAMPS

Dandelion, Large (Just For Fun)

Dandelion, Small (Just For Fun)

Pen Nib (Just For Fun)

INK PADS

Scarlet, ColorBox (Clearsnap)

Sunflower, ColorBox (Clearsnap)

clear embossing ink,
Top Boss (Clearsnap)

OTHER ITEMS

black mini journal

glue stick

bone folder

scissors

small photo slide mount

craft knife

cutting mat

gold embossing powder

heat gun

double-stick tape

foam tape

PAPER PREPARATION

$3^1/2$" x $5^1/4$" (9cm x 13cm)
2 pieces of white textured paper

$2^3/4$" x 4" (7cm x 10cm)
2 pieces of red mulberry paper

3" x 5" (8cm x 13cm)
red mulberry paper

vellum scraps

Y ou'll find a wide range of stampable objects in dollar stores! Here, a rather plain mini journal gets the royal treatment with some papers, inks and stamps, turning the ordinary into a lovely little gift.

one · On both of the textured white paper pieces, stamp the large Dandelion with the Scarlet ink about three times, making placement random. Fill in some of the space with three of the small Dandelions stamped in Sunflower on both pieces.

tip > Sometimes, foam tape can leave a sticky residue on your scissors. You can create your own non-stick coating by taking your clear embossing pad and wiping it across the blades prior to cutting the tape.

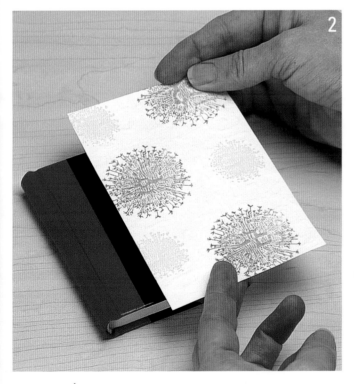

two · Apply glue stick to the outside of one of the journal covers and adhere one of the stamped papers about 1" (3cm) away from the spine. Smooth the paper down with the bone folder.

three · Using scissors, trim the corners of the papers away, leaving about 1/8" (3mm). Apply glue stick to the two side flaps and wrap them around the cover. Burnish the paper down with the bone folder.

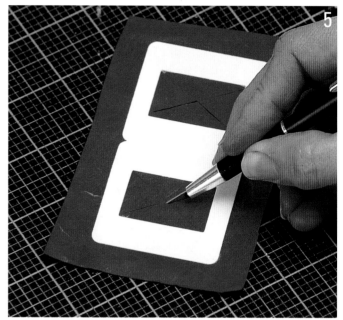

four · Apply glue to the last flap, wrap it around and burnish as before. Repeat steps two and three for the other cover of the journal. Apply glue stick to the inside of one cover and adhere one of the 2³/₄" x 4" (7cm x 10cm) red mulberry paper pieces.

five · Glue the second piece of mulberry paper to the other inside cover. Open up the slide mount and apply the glue stick to the outside. Lay the glued side down on the 3" x 5" (8cm x 13cm) piece of red mulberry paper. Use a craft knife and cutting mat to cut an X from corner to corner on both of the slide mount's openings.

*tip > Get in the habit of saving those cardstock scraps. You'll find it handy to have them separated into color families and filed in folders for easy access. And the scraps will be perfect for layering!

six · Add more glue around each slide mount opening and fold back the flaps created by the X. Burnish with the bone folder. Trim the outside corners of the mulberry paper and with another application of glue, wrap around the outside edges and burnish.

7

seven · With clear embossing ink, stamp the Pen Nib on a scrap of vellum and emboss with gold embossing powder. Secure the vellum to the inside of the slide mount with some double-stick tape. Add more double-stick tape to the inside of the slide mount and fold it closed to secure.

8

eight · Adhere pieces of foam tape to the back of the slide mount, avoiding the window area. Place the slide mount on the front of the mini journal.

ANOTHER SIMPLY BEAUTIFUL IDEA

This fabulous little journal was made in a snap. The journal was covered with Japanese Washi papers to create instant elegance. The gold-on-gold medallion on the front was made by simply stamping the image on gold cardstock and embossing with gold embossing powder. Cut the medallion out with deckle-edge scissors to avoid the fuss of cutting a perfectly circular shape!

surprise pocket folio

MATERIALS

STAMPS

Script Background (Inky Antics)

Heart Person (angi-b & co.)

Small Swirl Shapes Cube
(Alias Smith & Rowe)

INK PADS

Pink Grapefruit, VersaMagic (Tsukineko)

Turquoise Gem, VersaMagic (Tsukineko)

Frost White, ColorBox (Clearsnap)

OTHER ITEMS

stipple brush

$2^{3}/_{8}$" x $4^{3}/_{4}$" (6cm x 12cm)
manila shipping tag

white embossing powder

heat gun

deckle-edge scissors

foam tape

double-stick tape

decorative fibers

library pocket
(many rubber stamp stores carry these)

PAPER PREPARATION

blank CD folio (River City Rubber Works)

$1^{3}/_{4}$" x $3^{1}/_{2}$" (4cm x 9cm)
2 pieces of coral cardstock

$2^{1}/_{2}$" x 4" (6cm x 10cm)
2 pieces of white cardstock

$2^{1}/_{4}$" x 4" (6cm x 10cm)
dark coral cardstock

5" x 7" (13cm x 18cm)
coral cardstock

$5^{1}/_{8}$" x $5^{1}/_{8}$" (13cm x 13cm)
coral cardstock

This project is bound to inspire more ideas using a CD folder. You could make a wonderful gift by adding a CD you've burned with your favorite music!

one · Apply the Pink Grapefruit ink pad directly to the edges of the CD folio to create streaks of color. In single-direction strokes, smear on the ink (the application doesn't need to be too heavy). Also smear the ink on the slanted pocket inside the folio.

two · Randomly stamp the Script Background on the outside of the folio, using the Turquoise Gem ink pad. Do the same to the inside pocket. Stipple Pink Grapefruit over the entire front of the shipping tag, and then stamp the Script Background on it with the Turquoise Gem as well.

three · Stamp the Heart Person on both pieces of the 1³/₄" x 3¹/₂" (4cm x 9cm) coral cardstock using the Frost White ink pad, and emboss them with white embossing powder. Mount each piece on one of the white cardstock pieces and trim each piece closely with the deckle-edged scissors. Use foam tape to mount one figure onto the stippled and stamped tag and mount the other figure on the dark coral cardstock. Adhere the dark coral cardstock piece to the front of the folio with double-stick tape.

four · Thread the decorative fibers through the hole in the shipping tag and tie with a slip knot. Apply the Pink Grapefruit ink to the front of the library pocket in the same manner as in the cover of the CD folio from step one. Turn the pocket sideways so the opening is to your left. Randomly stamp swirl hearts from the Small Swirl Shapes cube in Turquoise Gem ink on the pocket. Slide the shipping tag into the pocket and set it aside. Open the folio and slide the 5" x 7" (13cm x 18cm) piece of coral cardstock inside the large left-side pocket. Slide it in as far as you can, then lift up the slanted pocket on the right and slip the coral cardstock under it. Pull the cardstock back under the slanted pocket so that it is about even with the right edge of the CD folio.

five · Randomly stamp the swirl hearts on the remaining piece of 5¹/₈" (13cm) square coral cardstock using the Frost White ink. With the CD folio open, use double-stick tape to adhere this piece on top of the left side pocket. Apply double-stick tape to the back of the library pocket and, with the pocket opening and the tag on the left side as shown, adhere the pocket to the stamped piece of coral cardstock.

heart folio

MATERIALS

STAMPS

Queen Anne's Lace (Just For Fun)

Sketchy Grid (Just For Fun)

Framed Swirl Heart (Just For Fun)

INK PADS

Lilac, ColorBox (Clearsnap)

Peony, ColorBox (Clearsnap)

OTHER ITEMS

sticky notes or scrap paper

stipple brush

stamp positioner (EK Success)

clear embossing powder

heat gun

deckle-edge scissors

double-stick tape

ruler

mini cutting mat

$^1/_8$" (3mm) hole punch

hammer

sheer magenta ribbon, 12" (30cm)

PAPER PREPARATION

Heart Folio card kit (The Paper Cut)

$3^3/_4$" x 4" (10cm x 10cm) white cardstock

$3^3/_4$" x 4" (10cm x 10cm) purple cardstock

G ive your heart to a loved one by creating this unique heart-shaped folio. It's featured here with a simple heart card inside, but you could easily fill the pocket with candies, photos, gift certificates or whatever your imagination can dream up.

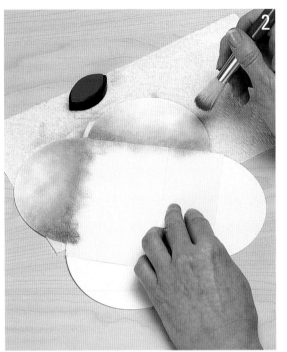

one · Open up the Heart Folio and randomly stamp the Queen Anne's Lace stamp four times over the heart portion, using the Lilac ink.

two · Turn the entire piece over and position sticky notes or scrap paper over the heart section. Use the stipple brush and Peony ink to apply color on the flaps, concentrating the color near the folds and fading it out toward the curved edges.

three · With the sticky notes or scrap paper still in place, use the stamp positioner to get the lines of the Sketchy Grid straight. Stamp the Sketchy Grid in Peony ink on the flaps.

four · Stamp the Framed Swirl Heart in Peony ink on the square of white cardstock. Emboss with clear embossing powder. Trim the embossed image with the deckle-edged scissors. Mount the embossed heart on the purple cardstock using double-stick tape. Close the flaps on the heart folio and from the bottom point, measure and mark two holes: one at 1½" (4cm) up from the point and the second at 2⅜" (6cm) up from the point. Insert the mini cutting mat behind the closed flaps and punch the two holes through the thicknesses of both flaps, using the hammer and the hole punch.

five · Thread the ribbon through the holes and tie it in front of the heart. Insert the embossed heart piece into the folio's pocket.

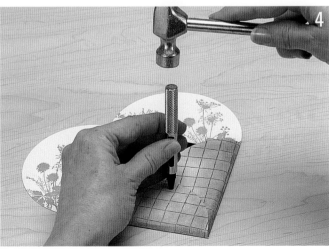

butterfly tag booklet

MATERIALS

STAMPS

Monarch Butterfly (Just For Fun)

INK PADS

Jet Black, Staz-On (Tsukineko)

Thatched Straw, VersaMagic (Tsukineko)

Key Lime, VersaMagic (Tsukineko)

Yellow Citrus, ColorBox (Clearsnap)

Rouge, ColorBox (Clearsnap)

Ice Jade, ColorBox (Clearsnap)

Blue Lagoon, ColorBox (Clearsnap)

Warm Violet, ColorBox (Clearsnap)

Tangerine, ColorBox (Clearsnap)

OTHER ITEMS

sticky notes, large

scissors

stipple brushes

Gelly Roll Glaze Pens (Sakura)

bone folder

ruler

$^1/_{16}$" (2mm) hole punch

double-stick tape

gold embroidery thread

floss threader

beads, 3

dragonfly charm

sheer ivory ribbon,
$^1/_4$" (6mm) wide and 21" (53cm) long

PAPER PREPARATION

$4^1/_8$" x $8^1/_2$" (11cm x 22cm)
manila shipping tag

$5^1/_2$" x $7^3/_8$" (14cm x 19cm)
colored paper for pocket page

$3^7/_8$" x $7^3/_8$" (10cm x 19cm)
colored papers for pages, 3 pieces

I magine the fun of receiving a clever little booklet made from a shipping tag, containing pages and pockets for little gifts and other treasures! Fill the pages with quotes, poetry, special recipes or just wonderful stamped images.

one · Stamp the Monarch Butterfly in Jet Black ink on the right half of the shipping tag. When the tag is folded in half, part of the left wing should be on the back. Stamp the butterfly on a sticky note and cut it out to create a mask. Place the mask over the butterfly on the tag. Using stipple brushes, stipple colors over the entire surface of the tag, blending each color into the next, similar to the gradation of a rainbow.

two · Remove the mask and color in the open areas of the butterfly using the gel pens.

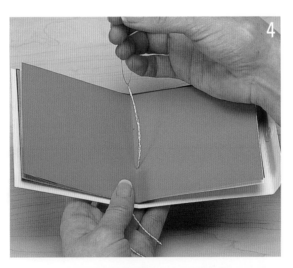

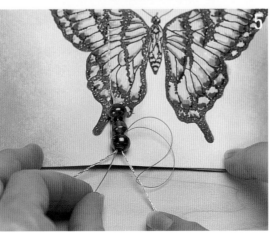

three · Turn the tag over. Using the bone folder and the ruler as a guide, score a line just below the shipping tag's hole. Fold on this line to create a flap and burnish with the bone folder. Fold the bottom of the tag up to the just-scored line and burnish along that fold as well.

four · Punch two ¹/₁₆" (2mm) holes, both about 1¹/₄" (3cm) from each edge of the tag along the second fold. Take the 5¹/₂" x 7³/₈" (14cm x 19cm) piece of colored paper and fold up the long edge 1⁵/₈" (4cm) to create a pocket. Use double-stick tape to tape the open ends together. Stack the rest of the colored papers on top and fold all in half to create the book's pages. Punch ¹/₁₆" (2mm) holes in these pages as was done for the cover. Place the pages inside the tag cover, lining up all the holes. Separate the embroidery thread into three strands and use the floss threader as a needle. Thread the floss from the outside of the tag cover, through all the holes of the pages, to the inside.

five · Come back through the second hole from the inside to the outside of the tag. Tie the two floss ends in a knot along the spine of the tag and thread on the beads and charm. Tie a knot through the last bead to secure. Tie the sheer ribbon through the shipping tag's hole with a slip knot and use it to secure the booklet closed.

flip-flop box

MATERIALS

STAMPS

Daisy (Just For Fun)

Small Swirl Shapes Cube
(Alias Smith & Rowe)

Mini Design Block Cube
(Just For Fun)

INK PADS

Jet Black, Staz-On (Tsukineko)

OTHER ITEMS

white shrink plastic

fine sand paper

Cut 'n Dry Brush Tip Pen Nibs (Ranger)

decorating chalks

scissors

small, shallow box lid (shoebox)

heat gun

wooden skewer

clear acrylic spray, glossy

papier mâché flip-flop box

foam brush

White, Bright Red acrylic paint (Delta
Ceramcoat)

craft glue or super glue

Craft stores have an abundance of papier mâché items, including these cute flip-flop sandal boxes! Dress one up with some paint and a shrink plastic charm to create a fun gift box.

1

one · Prepare the shrink plastic by sanding it six or seven times crosswise, then again lengthwise. Stamp the Daisy on the plastic using the Jet Black ink. Use the pen nib applicators to apply decorative chalks to the Daisy.

tip > Shrink plastic can be colored any number of ways, both before and after shrinking. Colored pencils, permanent markers and mica powders all provide great results. There are even some brands that can be run through your inkjet printer prior to shrinking. Acrylic paints and markers can be used on pieces that have already been shrunk.

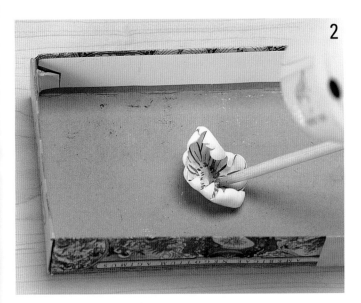

2

two · Cut the colored daisy out with scissors, taking care not to smear the chalks. Trim closely to the image and cut the stem off entirely. Place the shrink plastic piece in the cardboard lid and shrink it with the heat gun, using the wooden skewer to gently secure it. Don't panic when the plastic begins to curl up—that's normal and it will uncurl as it completes its shrinkage.

3

three · When the plastic appears to have finished shrinking, turn off the heat gun and immediately flatten the plastic with the flat, wood side of a rubber stamp. Spray clear acrylic spray over the finished piece and set it aside.

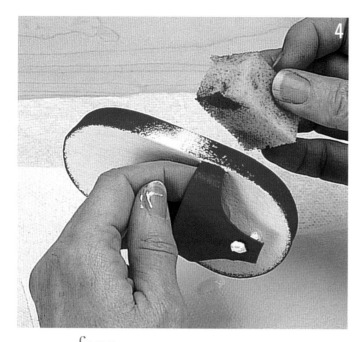

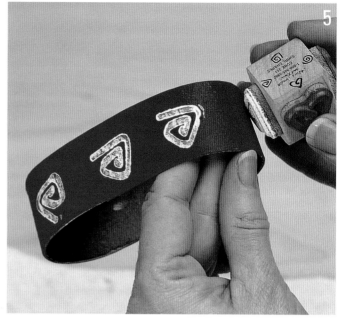

four · Using a foam brush, paint the exterior of the box and its lid white. You may need to apply a second coat. Once the paint has dried, paint the box with Bright Red. Paint the sides of the lid and the thong portion Bright Red as well. Rinse out the brush.

five · After the red paint is dry, dab white paint onto the triangle swirl side of the Small Swirl Shapes cube, using a foam brush. Stamp the triangle swirl repeatedly around the outside of the box. Keep one hand inside the box to create pressure from the inside when stamping against it.

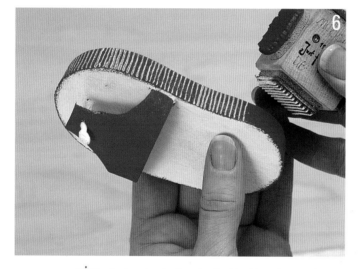

six · Again, using the foam brush, dab white paint onto the parallel lines side of the Mini Design Block Cube and stamp vertical lines around the perimeter of the lid's side.

seven · To finish, glue the daisy onto the center of the top of the thong with craft or super glue.

tip > Whenever using acrylic paint on a rubber stamp, be sure to immediately clean the stamp after stamping, to prevent the paint from drying on the rubber die.

ANOTHER SIMPLY BEAUTIFUL IDEA

Stamp artist Sandy Sandrus created this tropical pin. After sanding clear shrink plastic, she stamped the sunset and used colored pencils on the opposite side of the plastic to color in the images. The beach chair and umbrella were stamped and colored on separate pieces of clear shrink plastic. After all pieces were cut out and shrank, she assembled the piece by layering the chair and umbrella on the sunset scene using a strong craft adhesive. Finally, Sandy added a pin on the back.

ANOTHER SIMPLY BEAUTIFUL IDEA

Here's another idea from Sandy; a card and gift in one! Shrink plastic flip-flop pins were made by simply drawing a flip-flop pattern and tracing it on white shrink plastic. She used several colors of ink to stamp the swirl designs on the surface of the flip-flops, cut them out, punched two holes for the thongs on each and shrank them with a heat gun. She also stamped a flower and used a matching punch to punch it from the shrink plastic, then shrank it. A piece of 26-gauge wire was cut and attached at one of the side holes, then threaded with seed beads. The same piece was attached at the toe area, threaded with more beads, and then finished by attaching at the opposite side hole. The flower was attached with strong craft glue.

floral notebook

MATERIALS

STAMPS

Webbed and Spattered Background
(Just For Fun)

Tulip Silhouette (Just For Fun)

Fluffy Flower Silhouette (Just For Fun)

Lily Silhouette (Just For Fun)

"Journal" (Just For Fun)

INK PADS

Pink Grapefruit,
VersaMagic (Tsukineko)

English Red,
Marvy Matchable No. 28 (Uchida)

OTHER ITEMS

9³/₄" (25cm) length of blue Magic Mesh

composition book

scissors

18" (46cm) length of red gingham ribbon,
¹/₂" (12mm) wide

glue stick

corner rounder punch

double-stick tape

watercolor crayons

fine mist spray bottle

foam tape

PAPER PREPARATION

9³/₄" x 6³/₄" (25cm x 17cm)
2 pieces of cream cardstock

6³/₄" x 4¹/₂" (17cm x 11cm)
red textured cardstock

watercolor paper scraps

1" x 4" (3cm x 10cm)
cream cardstock

1¹/₄" x 4¹/₄" (3cm x 11cm)
blue cardstock

Transfer a lowly composition book into a work of art! By covering it with cardstock and adding a few embellishments, you can have a beautiful journal.

one · Cut a piece of Magic Mesh the length of the spine of the composition book. Peel off the backing and center it on the spine, wrapping it around from one side to the other.

two · Trim the ribbon to five lengths of about 3½" (9cm) each. Apply double-stick tape or glue stick to the back of each and wrap them around the spine, spacing them evenly.

*tip > Directly coloring on rubber dies with watercolor crayons or water-based markers is a fun way to create a fluid, watercolor effect. After stamping the first impression, spray again with a mist of water and stamp for a pale, delicate look.

three · Trim two pieces of cream cardstock to fit the front and back covers of the journal, leaving about ¾" (19mm) of the decorated spine exposed. If the corners of the journal are rounded, use a corner rounder punch on the cover pieces. Stamp over the entire surface of both pieces using the Pink Grapefruit ink and the Webbed and Spattered Background. Apply glue to the back of each piece with the glue stick and adhere to the covers.

four · Use double-stick tape to adhere the red textured cardstock to the center of the front of the book and set aside. Directly color on the flower stamps rubber die with the watercolor crayons.

five · Spray the colored stamp with a fine mist of water. Be careful not to make it too wet; it should glisten but not be runny.

six · Stamp the flower onto the watercolor paper.

seven · Repeat, using a variety of flower stamps, for a total of five flowers. Cut out each flower with scissors, leaving a small border. Use the glue stick to adhere them in a row on the red card-stock on the cover of the book. Stamp the *Journal* stamp onto a scrap of cream cardstock in English Red ink. Use double-stick tape to layer this piece to the blue cardstock and, using foam tape, adhere it to the front of the book in the bottom right corner of the red cardstock on the cover.

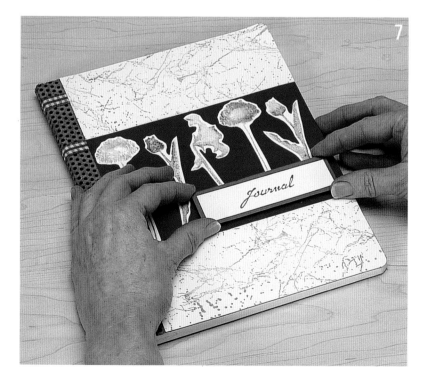

ANOTHER SIMPLY BEAUTIFUL IDEA

To create a "shabby chic" look, for this gardener's journal the spine was painted first with white acrylic paint, then green, and then wiped with a paper towel while still wet. White cardstock was stamped and adhered to the covers and a pretty floral ribbon was added along the spine's edge. Flower silhouettes were stamped on another piece of white cardstock using the same colors from the journal's cover pieces, then layered on turquoise cardstock to create the panel for the title. Stick-on letters spell out the word *Journal*.

ANOTHER SIMPLY BEAUTIFUL IDEA

Once you start covering composition books, you won't want to stop! This travel journal was put together easily by first covering the book with a textured cardstock. A passport stamp background was stamped and embossed repeatedly along a strip of white cardstock. Choosing colors that coordinate with the cardstock covers, the background was painted lightly with watercolors and attached along the journal's spine. Adding some stamped and gold-embossed passports along with the words *Travel Journal* completes the project.

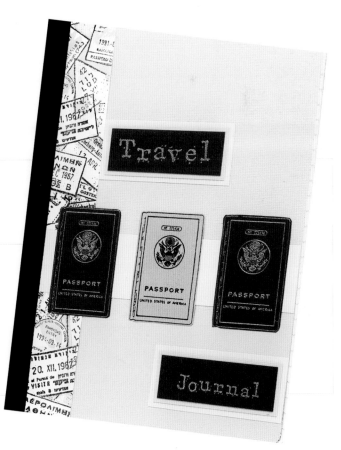

travel concertina

MATERIALS

STAMPS

Tree Line (Just For Fun)

Evergreen (Just For Fun)

Unmounted Alphabet (Just For Fun)

INK PADS

Meadow, Adirondack (Ranger)

Starfish Green, Sea Shells (Ranger)

Jet Black, Staz-On (Tsukineko)

OTHER ITEMS

scissors

double-stick tape

black photo corners (Xyron)

glue stick

bone folder

$1/4$" (6mm) wide satin ribbon

beads

floss threader

vellum tape

five photos

deckle-edged scissors

PAPER PREPARATION

$3^{3}/_{4}$" x $9^{3}/_{4}$" (10cm x 25cm)
3 pieces of tan art paper, charcoal-weight

tan scrap for title

scraps of red and teal cardstocks for
photo and title layering

$2^{7}/_{8}$" x $4^{1}/_{4}$" (7cm x 11cm)
matboard scraps

$4^{1}/_{4}$" x $5^{3}/_{4}$" (11cm x 15cm)
soft green handmade paper, 2 pieces

$8^{1}/_{2}$" x 11" (22cm x 28cm)
sheet of vellum

What better way to create a memory of a loved one's visit than to make a mini photo album for them, compiled of photos to capture all of the memories! This little scrapbook will surely be cherished by the recipient as a reminder of your great times together.

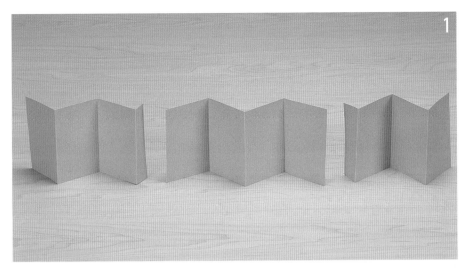

one · Fold one piece of the long tan paper in half, widthwise, then fold each end back in the opposite direction to form an accordion. Repeat with the other two pieces of tan paper. On two of the pieces, cut off enough paper from one end of each piece to leave a 1" (3cm) flap. Connect the three pieces together with double-stick tape, adhering the flaps of the two outside pieces to the ends of the center piece.

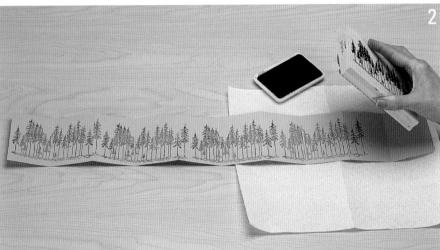

two · Stamp the Tree Line stamp down the entire length of the concertina, using the Meadow ink. Try to keep the image aligned straight.

tip > Charcoal paper comes in many different colors and is usually about the same weight as cardstock. It is available in larger sheets, so if you don't wish to cut and join several pieces of cardstock to form a concertina (accordion) this may be a good paper choice for you.

three · Set the concertina aside. Stamp the Evergreen stamp in Starfish Green ink on the small scrap of tan paper for the cover title. Without re-inking the stamp, stamp the image two more times to create lighter images. Re-ink the stamp and repeat once more.

four · Stamp out the title of your album onto the scrap of tan cardstock with the Unmounted Alphabet and the Jet Black ink. An easy way to handle small, unmounted dies is to wrap a piece of double-stick tape around your finger and stick each letter to your finger as you ink and stamp it. Don't be too concerned with lining up the letters perfectly; the look should be loose.

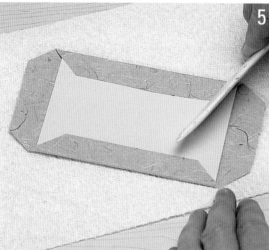

*tip > Photo corners are a great way to mount not only photos but also pieces of text. Some photo corners are self-adhesive and some require you to moisten the back before adhering, just like an envelope. Look for corners that are acid-free. You'll find many colors available at scrapbooking stores, including some great metallics.

five · Use the black photo corners to secure the title piece to a small piece of teal cardstock. Set this piece aside. Spread the glue stick over one side of one of the matboard covers. Place it glue side down on top of one piece of the handmade paper. Trim the corners of the handmade paper. Spread more glue over the two long flaps and wrap the paper around the board, burnishing with the bone folder.

six · Glue the short flaps and burnish in the same manner. Repeat the gluing process for the other board. Trim the ribbon to one length of 20" (51cm) and a second length of 16" (41cm). Secure the ribbon with double-stick tape to one long side of each of the covered boards. Apply double-stick tape to the back of the first and last panels of the concertina and adhere each end to each board. Be sure the ribbons are positioned as shown.

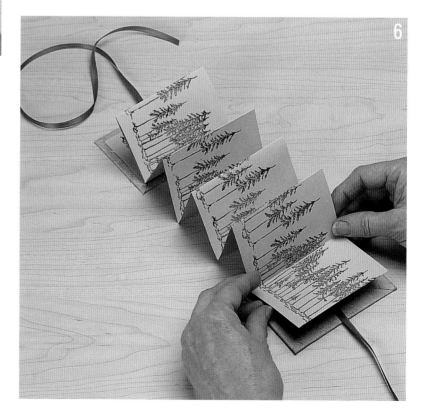

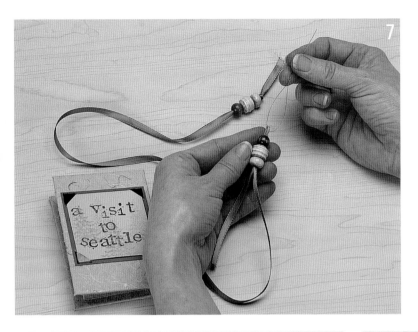

seven · Attach the title piece to the front of the album, using double-stick tape. Thread three beads on each ribbon, using the floss threader as a needle, and tie an overhand knot at each end to secure.

eight · Typeset all of the journaling for the photos on a computer, then print them out on the sheet of vellum (be sure the printer ink has dried before handling the vellum). Individually tear out each journaling entry. Use the vellum tape to adhere one entry to every other page.

nine · Crop your five photos, if necessary, to fit on the individual pages and use double-stick tape to layer them on red cardstock. Trim with deckle-edged scissors.

ten · Layer the photos on teal cardstock and use double-stick tape to adhere the photos to the remaining pages in the album. Tie the album closed by taking the longer ribbon and wrapping it around the album once, then tie it in front with the other ribbon.

photo cd folio

MATERIALS

STAMPS

Postcard Background (Just For Fun)

"Travel" (Just For Fun)

Design Block, Square and Frame
1³/₄" x 1³/₄" (4cm x 4cm) (Just For Fun)

Design Block, Square and Frame
1" x 1" (3cm x 3cm) (Just For Fun)

Passport Collage (Just For Fun)

Customs Border (Just For Fun)

INK PADS

Yellow Citrus, ColorBox (Clearsnap)

French Blue, ColorBox (Clearsnap)

Jet Black, Staz-On (Tsukineko)

Thatched Straw, VersaMagic (Tsukineko)

Peach Pastel, ColorBox (Clearsnap)

OTHER ITEMS

one large photo slide mount

waterbrush

glue stick

bone folder

double-stick tape

deckle-edged scissors

photos

foam tape

PAPER PREPARATION

blank CD folio (River City Rubber Works)

2⁵/₈" x 5¹/₈" (7cm x 13cm)
blue mulberry paper

5" x 7" (13cm x 18cm)
blue cardstock

5¹/₈" x 10" (13cm x 25cm)
cream cardstock

blue cardstock scraps for layering photos

H ere's a great idea for a gift: Burn a CD with photos and give it to the recipient in a CD folder that you've decorated with rubber stamps! This particular folio was decorated to reflect the travel theme of some memorable vacation photographs.

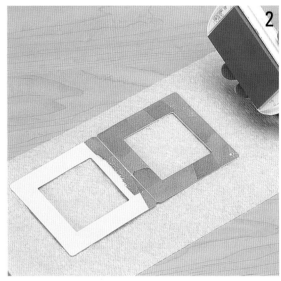

one · Streak the Yellow Citrus ink onto the front of the CD folio and the inside slanted pocket by applying the ink pad directly to the cardstock. Concentrate the color along the edges of the folio. Ink the Postcard Background with French Blue ink and stamp onto the front and back panels and the inside slanted pocket of the CD folio. It's not necessary to stamp around the spine area; that will be covered later.

two · With the French Blue ink pad, apply color directly to one side of the slide mount, completely covering it with color.

three · Stamp "Travel" onto the bottom edge of the inked side of the slide mount, using the Jet Black ink, and set it aside. On one long edge of the mulberry paper, paint a line of water using the waterbrush (or a regular paintbrush dipped in water). Tear the paper along this water line to achieve a nice feathered edge. Repeat for the other long side of the mulberry paper. Cover one side of the torn mulberry paper with glue stick and adhere it to the outside spine of the CD folio. Smooth the paper down with the bone folder.

four · Line the slanted pocket on the inside of the folio with the large piece of blue cardstock and secure it with double-stick tape (see step 4 on page 97). Fold the cream cardstock in half to make a card. Randomly stamp the shadow side of the larger Design Block in Thatched Straw in a "tumbling" pattern over the front and inside panels of the cream cardstock. Repeat with the Peach Pastel using the smaller Design Block shadow.

five · With the French Blue ink, randomly stamp over the shadow stamping with the Passport Collage and the Customs Border stamps. Mount your photos on blue cardstock scraps and trim closely with the deckle-edged scissors. Apply double-stick tape to the back unstamped panel of the cream cardstock. Attach it to the left inside panel of the CD folio, with the cream cardstock's fold to your left. Adhere your photos to all three decorated panels of the cream cardstock, using double-stick tape. Place one photo inside the slide mount and fold the two sides together, using double-stick tape to adhere it. Attach the slide mount to the front of the folio with foam tape.

holiday favor cube

MATERIALS

STAMPS

Tree Cube (Just For Fun)

Ornament Cube (Just For Fun)

INK PADS

Frost White, ColorBox (Clearsnap)

OTHER ITEMS

bone folder

ruler

double-stick tape

glittery white embossing powder

heat gun

deckle-edged scissors

gold leafing pen

PAPER PREPARATION

2$\frac{1}{2}$" x 10$\frac{1}{2}$" (6cm x 27cm)
light green cardstock

2$\frac{1}{2}$" x 10$\frac{1}{2}$" (6cm x 27cm)
white cardstock

2" x 2" (5cm x 5cm)
6 pieces of dark green cardstock

1$\frac{7}{8}$" x 1$\frac{7}{8}$" (5cm x 5cm)
2 pieces of white cardstock

1$\frac{7}{8}$" x 1$\frac{7}{8}$" (5cm x 5cm)
2 pieces of red cardstock

2" x 2" (5cm x 5cm)
4 pieces of red cardstock

Here's another idea from stamp artist Sandy Sandrus. Decorate your holiday table with these clever cubes, hiding little gifts inside each one! Or pile them up as a centerpiece. Whatever the occasion, you'll find lots of uses for making these cubes—they're easily assembled, too!

one · On the light green strip of cardstock, measure and score every 2½" (6cm), using the bone folder and ruler as a guide; a ½" (12mm) flap will be left at the end. Fold along all the scored lines to create a box shape. Place a piece of double-stick tape on the end flap and connect the two ends together.

two · Repeat the scoring and folding process for the white cardstock strip. Slide the white box into the light green box to create a cube.

*tip > When you need to make several cuts or scores that are perpendicular with the edge of the paper, try using a cutting mat that has a grid printed on it and a see-through ruler. Just line up the top edge of the paper with a line on the grid, and align the vertical lines of the ruler with those on the grid. This saves time over having to mark both sides of the paper.

three · Stamp and emboss each of the trees from the Tree Cube onto four 2" (5cm) squares of dark green cardstock, stamping with the Frost White and embossing with the glittery white embossing powder. Trim about ⅛" (3mm) off of each tree piece with the deckle-edged scissors.

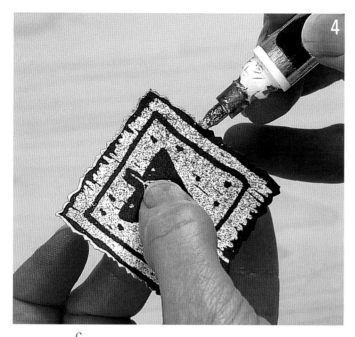

four · Use the gold leafing pen to gild the edges of each tree piece. Set these aside to dry.

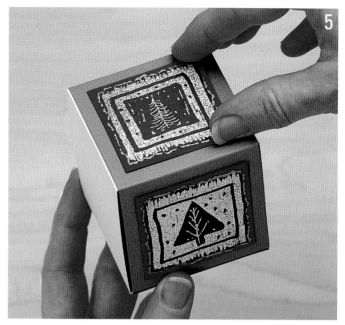

five · Layer each tree piece to a 2" (5cm) square of red cardstock with double-stick tape. Mount each layered tree onto the green sides of the cube. Trees on opposite sides of one another should be right-side up.

six · Stamp and emboss two ornaments from the Ornament Cube onto the two pieces of 1⅞" (5cm) red cardstock, using the Frost White ink and the glittery white embossing powder. Trim off about ⅛" (3mm) around the edges of each with the deckle-edged scissors, and gild with the gold leafing pen, just as you did before with the tree pieces. Mount the gilded pieces on the two squares of white cardstock using double-stick tape. Attach these with more tape onto the last two 2" (5cm) squares of dark green cardstock.

seven · Mount the two ornament squares onto the two remaining sides of the cube.

ANOTHER SIMPLY BEAUTIFUL IDEA

Keep your party coordinated by creating the invitation with the same cardstocks and motifs used in making the Holiday Favor Cubes! This invitation features one tree and one ornament from the cube lined up side-by-side and placed on the front of the card. Using the same embossing powders, gold leaf edging and layers as used on the cube, it makes a perfect match for the favors.

ANOTHER SIMPLY BEAUTIFUL IDEA

Sandy Sandrus made these adorable baby blocks to serve as the centerpiece for a baby shower. She used pastel colors of cardstock along with large alphabet stamps (Hot Potatoes) and baby-inspired stamp images (Art Gone Wild!) to create the very same blocks with a very different look!

dreidel candy box

MATERIALS

STAMPS

Square Box Template (Inky Antics)

Striped Background (Just For Fun)

Sketchy Dreidel (Ruth's Jewish Stamps)

Jewish Border (Ruth's Jewish Stamps)

INK PADS

any light-colored dye ink

French Blue, ColorBox (Clearsnap)

OTHER ITEMS

scissors

craft knife

ruler

cutting mat

bone folder

stamp positioner (EK Success)

double-stick tape

3" x 3" (8cm x 8cm) clear acetate

sticky note

foam tape

PAPER PREPARATION

5½" x 5¾" (14cm x 15cm)
3 pieces of white cardstock

Before you spin the dreidel for Hanukkah, put together one of these boxes for each of the participants for storing their gold coins! The box is easy to make, with the help of another great template stamp from Inky Antics.

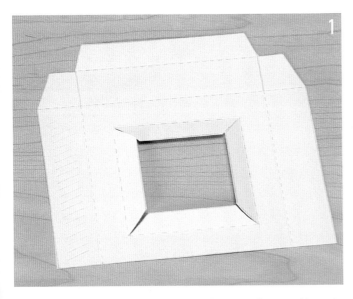

one • Stamp the Square Box Template twice onto white card-stock, inking up the window section for only one of the stamped images, and using a light-colored ink. Cut out each box shape. With a craft knife and ruler, remove the window portion from one of the stamped templates. Use a bone folder and ruler to score along all of the dotted lines on both box images. Cut on the solid, mitered corner lines of the window and fold the sides inward.

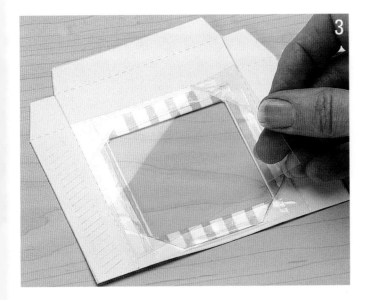

two • Turn the stamped box parts over and use the stamp positioner to align and stamp the Striped Background in French Blue over the entire surface.

three • Fold along all of the scored lines and burnish with the bone folder. Secure the flaps around the window with double-stick tape and burnish. Apply more tape on top of the taped-down flaps and adhere the piece of acetate.

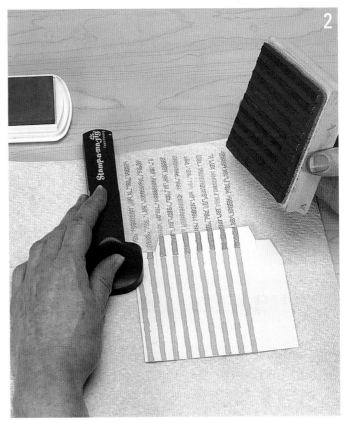

*tip > You may find that, after filling the box with candy, the bottom may need reinforcement! Use double-stick tape to tape the bottom flap in place.

four · Use double-stick tape to adhere the side flaps on one box image to the other to form a complete box. Fold in the flaps at the top and the bottom to close the box.

five · Stamp the box image one more time on the white card-stock, without inking the window section. Cut off all flaps from around the large middle square except for the flap on the left side.

six · Cover the square portion with a sticky note or scrap piece of paper and stamp the Striped Background on the flap section using the French Blue ink.

*tip >

When cutting a mask, be sure to keep the scissors cutting just inside the image's outline. This will help to avoid the dreaded "halo" effect when stamping on top of the mask.

seven · Stamp the Sketchy Dreidel in French Blue on the remaining white square. Score along the dotted line, fold and apply double-stick tape to the back of the striped portion. Adhere it to the side of the box.

eight · Stamp the Jewish Border stamp onto white cardstock in French Blue and cut apart four of the individual elements. Adhere them in a vertical line to the left side of the front of the box, using foam tape.

ANOTHER SIMPLY BEAUTIFUL IDEA

This box was created by using the same Square Box Template and Striped Background stamps. No extra cover was added to the front of this box. Instead, it was embellished with holly leaf cutouts and a few holly berry "jewels"!

I encourage you to support your local rubber stamp and scrapbooking stores whenever possible! If you can't find an item you're looking for, contact the manufacturer for a retailer near you.

resources

ALIAS SMITH & ROWE

3110 Payne Avenue

Cleveland, OH 44114

(800) 945-3980

www.asrstamps.com

• *rubber stamps*

AMERICAN TOMBOW, INC.

355 Satellite Boulevard NE

Suite 300

Suwanee, GA 30024

www.tombowusa.com

• *colored markers*

ANGIE-B & COMPANY

2418 N. 11th Street

Clinton, IA 52732

(563) 243-1151

www.angi-b-co.com

• *rubber stamps*

ART GONE WILD!

3110 Payne Avenue

Cleveland, OH 44114

(800) 945-3980

www.agwstamps.com

• *rubber stamps*

BAZZILL BASICS PAPER

701 N. Golden Key Street

Gilbert, AZ 85233

(480) 558-8557

www.bazzillbasics.com

• *assorted papers*

CLEARSNAP, INC.

P.O. Box 98

Anacortes, WA 98221

(888) 448-4862

www.clearsnap.com

• *inks and ink pads*

DELTA TECHNICAL COATINGS, INC.

Whittier, CA 90601

(800) 423-4135

www.deltacrafts.com

• *acrylic paints*

EK SUCCESS

www.eksuccess.com

• *stamp positioner*

FISKARS

7811 W. Stewart Avenue

Wausau, WI 54401

(800) 500-4849

www.fiskars.com

• *decorative-edged scissors, paper cutters, trimmers*

INKY ANTICS

3110 Payne Avenue

Cleveland, OH 44114

(800) 945-3980

www.inkyantics.com

• *rubber stamps*

JUST FOR FUN RUBBER STAMPS

301 E. Lemon Street, Suite A-B

Tarpon Springs, FL 34689

(727) 938-9898

www.jffstamps.com

• *rubber stamps*

KRYLON, INC.

www.krylon.com

• *leafing pens, spray finishes*

LUCKY SQUIRREL

P.O. Box 606

Belen, NM 87002

(800) 462-4912

www.luckysquirrel.com

• *shrink plastic*

LUMINARTE

3322 W. Sussex Way

Fresno, CA 93722

(866) 229-1544

www.luminarteinc.com

• *Radiant Pearls, Twinkling H2O's*

MAGIC MESH

P. O. Box 8

Lake City, MN 55041

(651) 345-6374

www.magicmesh.com

• *mesh trim*

**MARCO PRINTED PRODUCTS
COMPANY, INC.**
14 Marco Lane
Centerville, OH 45458
(888) 433-5239
www.marcopaper.com
• *assorted papers and cards*

MARVY UCHIDA
Uchida of America, Corp.
3535 Del Amo Boulevard
Torrance, CA 90503
(800) 541-5877
www.marvy.com
• *inks and ink pads*

THE PAPER CUT
234 W. Northland Avenue
Appleton, WI 54911
(920) 954-6210
www.thepapercut.com
• *prefolded cards*

RANGER INDUSTRIES
15 Park Road
Tinton Falls, NJ 07724
(732) 389-3535
www.rangerink.com
• *inks and ink pads*

RIVER CITY RUBBER WORKS
5555 South Meridian
Wichita, KS 67217
(877) 735-2276
www.rivercityrubberworks.com
• *CD folios*

RUBBER STAMPEDE
Berkeley, CA 94701
(800) 423-4135
www.rubberstampede.com
• *rubber stamps*

RUTH'S JEWISH STAMPS
3703 Tunbridge Wells SE
Salem, OR 97302
www.ruthsjewishstamps.com
• *rubber stamps*

SAKURA OF AMERICA, INC.
www.gellyroll.com
• *gel pens*

3M CORPORATE HEADQUARTERS
3M Center
St. Paul, MN 55144
(888) 3M-HELPS
www.3m.com
• *tapes and adhesives*

TSUKINEKO, INC.
17640 NE 65th Street
Redmond, WA 98052 USA
(425) 883-7733
www.tsukineko.com
• *inks and ink pads*

index

THE BEST IN CREATIVE INSTRUCTION AND INSPIRATION IS FROM NORTH LIGHT BOOKS!

• THESE BOOKS AND OTHER FINE NORTH LIGHT TITLES are available from your local art & craft retailer, bookstore or online supplier.

SIMPLY BEAUTIFUL GREETING CARDS

Whether you're a complete beginner or a seasoned crafter, *Simply Beautiful Greeting Cards* shows you how to create personalized greeting cards for every occasion. In addition to the wide array of cards, you'll find a helpful section on basic tools and materials as well as a treasure trove of papercrafting tips and tricks.

ISBN-13: 978-1-58180-564-2

ISBN-10: 1-58180-564-0, paperback, 128 pages, #33019

30-MINUTE RUBBER STAMP WORKSHOP

Create a wonderful, personal gift in the time it takes to drive to the store! In *30-Minute Rubber Stamp Workshop*, Sandra McCall shows you how to handcraft gorgeous rubber stamped pieces without taking all day to do it. Through full-color illustrations and clear, step-by-step instructions, you'll be making wonderful creations in no time.

ISBN-13: 978-1-58180-271-9

ISBN-10: 1-58180-271-4, paperback, 128 pages, #32142

TEXTURE EFFECTS FOR RUBBER STAMPING

Crafters can satisfy their craving for texture with this treasure trove of 37 elegant card and gift projects. Inside, you'll find an abundance of texture-making techniques, including stamping with metallic paints, resist effects, alcohol inks, layers of acetate, watercolors and embellishments. *Texture Effects for Rubber Stamping* is an inspirational resource that crafters will turn to time after time.

ISBN-13: 978-1-58180-558-1

ISBN-10: 1-58180-558-6, paperback, 128 pages, #33014

STAMPING FUN FOR BEGINNERS

This is an indispensable, user-friendly handbook for newcomers as well as a great quick-reference guide for seasoned artists. This must-have book features projects, like greeting cards, gift tags, boxes, jewelry and journals. It's also filled to the brim with dozens of techniques, including embossing, layering, making your own stamps and more!

ISBN-13: 978-1-58180-585-7

ISBN-10: 1-58180-585-3, paperback, 128 pages, #33054